LEGENDS OF THE WEST SERIES

WASHINGTON

MYTHS & LEGENDS

THE TRUE STORIES BEHIND HISTORY'S MYSTERIES

SECOND EDITION

L. E. BRAGG

TWODOT®

GUILFORD, CONNECTICUT
HELENA, MONTANA

A · TWODOT® · BOOK

An imprint and registered trademark of Rowman & Littlefield

Distributed by NATIONAL BOOK NETWORK

British Library Cataloguing-in-Publication Information available

Library of Congress Cataloging-in-Publication Data

Bragg, L. E. (Lynn E.), 1956-
  Washington myths & legends : the true stories behind history's mysteries / L.E. Bragg.
      pages cm. — (Legends of the West series)
  Includes bibliographical references and index.
    ISBN 978-1-4930-1603-7 (paperback : alkaline paper)—ISBN 978-1-4930-1604-4 (ebook) 1. Tales—Washington (State) 2. Legends—Washington (State) 3. Washington (State)—Social life and customs—Anecdotes. 4. Washington (State)—History, Local—Anecdotes. 5. Washington (State)—Biography—Anecdotes. 6. Curiosities and wonders—Washington (State)—Anecdotes. I. Title.
  GR110.W3B735 2015
  398.209797—dc23

                                                                    2015017294

CONTENTS

We have to accept the possibility that we may never know.
I guess we can live with that, if we have to.

—FBI Agent (ret.), Ralph Himmelsbach,
referring to D. B. Cooper,
The Columbian, November 22, 1996

ACKNOWLEDGMENTS

Special thanks to:

My editors, Megan Hiller and Courtney Oppel;

Jim Marich, a docent at The Museum of Flight and WWII veteran who served as a second lieutenant and flight engineer on a B-29 bomber, for his knowledge of historic airplanes;

Ralph Himmelsbach and Larry Finegold, for their D. B. Cooper expertise and experiences;

Petter Pettersen and Ray McWade, for sharing details of their lives in the Georgetown Castle;

Fred Pflugrath, editor—*Appleland Bulletin*;

Jody Gripp, NW Room—Tacoma Public Library;

Librarians at the University of Victoria;

Lisa Werner—UW Alumni Association;

Nancy Gale Compau and Rayette Sterling—Spokane Public Library's Northwest History Room;

Barbara G. Kenady-Fish—Public Affairs & Special Projects, Okanogan & Wenatchee National Forest Service;

Evelyn L. Arnold, Chelan County auditor, and the clerks at the Chelan County Recorder's Office;

Carol Schultz, Chelan County Superior Court clerk;

Gregory Lauder-Frost, Scottish genealogist;

Steve and Kathy Christensen, for sharing their personal experiences with me;

Carolyn Marr—Museum of History and Industry;

Ray Dong and the patient librarians at the Seattle Public Library;

Alyssa Burrows and Eric Flom—HistoryLink.org;

Dede Wilhelm—Boise researcher;

And, as always, Polly Bragg, for reading and editing everything!

PREFACE

Nestled in the furthest Northwestern corner of the continental United States, Washington has long been steeped in myth and mystery. Northwest Indian legends have involved spirits for thousands of years. Puget Sound area tribes revered the spirit world, and tribes along the Columbia River worshiped ghosts through their art and oral traditions to the extent that anthropologist William Duncan Strong described them as a ghost cult. Captain William Clark of the Lewis and Clark Expedition wrote of the "peculiar fascination with spirits by the Indians of the region" (William Arnold, *Seattle Post-Intelligencer*, 31 October 1976).

Ancient Indian myths also tell of shadowy beings such as sea serpents and the Seeahtic tribe of giant, hairy beasts, also known in some parts of the continent as Sasquatch. Early miners and settlers saw these mysterious creatures, and sightings continue to this day.

From Puget Sound to the Inland Empire, tales of buried treasure and unsolved events abound. The mysteries in this book have their roots in the early days of Washington, most before 1940. Since Washington's most famous unsolved mystery is that of skyjacker D. B. Cooper, I begin with his 1971 story. I end the book with the story of a man who lived more than 9,000 years ago but is controversial to this day. The book is filled with diverse stories of crime, ghosts, treasure and unexplained phenomena from both sides of the Cascade Mountains.

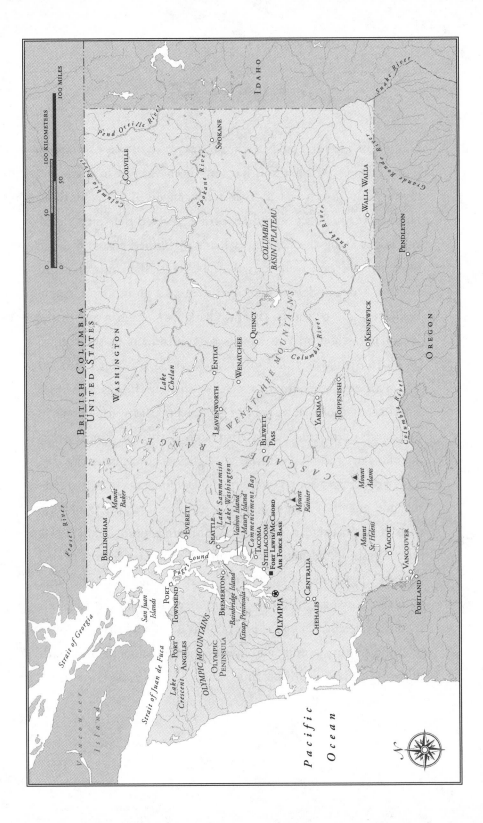

D. B. COOPER,
WHERE ARE YOU?

Eight-year-old Brian Ingram was digging in the sand on Tena Bar along the shores of the Columbia River when he made a discovery that would reactivate an investigation into a nine-year-old unsolved Northwest mystery. Ingram and his family were on a winter excursion and Sunday picnic February 10, 1980, along a sandy Columbia River beach just a few miles downriver from Vancouver and the Interstate 5 bridge over the river. Ingram was digging a hole for a fire pit when he uncovered a soggy, half-disintegrated pack of twenty-dollar bills just inches below ground, under a shallow layer of sand. The family turned the money, a sum of $5,800, in to local authorities, who contacted the Federal Bureau of Investigation. The bills were so rotten that only Andrew Jackson's image and the serial numbers were visible. A check of the serial numbers revealed that the bills were from the United States' only unsolved skyjacking case. Young Ingram had found the only tangible clue in the investigation since the hijacking.

———

Thanksgiving eve, November 24, 1971, was a typical Northwest November day, full of wind and rain. No one noticed when "Dan Cooper" walked up to the Northwest Orient Airlines ticket counter at Portland International Airport and paid cash for a one-way ticket from Portland to Seattle. Nor did anyone pay attention to the average-looking, middle-aged man as he sat among the Thanksgiving travelers for fifty minutes waiting for his flight. The quiet man was an olive-skinned, slender white male with dark hair parted on the left and a receding hairline. He wore a black suit with a white shirt and narrow black tie under a black raincoat. His shoes were brown loafers. Later on, during the flight, he sported dark, wrap-around sunglasses.

Around 3:00 p.m. the Boeing 727 took off from Portland bound for Seattle. The nondescript passenger sat in seat 18c, near the back of the plane. No one else sat with him in the last row of seats in the coach compartment. He drank several whiskeys and chain smoked Raleigh cigarettes. Not long after takeoff he passed a note to the flight attendant. Thinking it contained some sort of pickup line, the flight attendant pocketed the folded piece of paper. In response to her rebuff, the man in 18c advised, "Miss, you'd better look at that note. I have a bomb." The note did not ask for her phone number as she thought it might. Rather, the message said that the man had a bomb with him, the pilot should wait for further instructions and there should be "no funny stuff." When the flight crew learned of the matter, they radioed ground control to advise them of the situation.

The flight attendant was instructed to try to determine whether Cooper really had a bomb on board. When she queried him, he opened his briefcase just long enough for her to see red cylinders and a tangle of wires that filled the suitcase. Cooper continued to communicate with the attendant through a series of preprinted notes. He asked for four parachutes and $200,000 in unmarked bills. He would allow the plane to land in Seattle and the other passengers to disembark in exchange for the money and parachutes. The hijacker told the woman that he would be able to recognize Tacoma from the air, and he knew that McChord Air Force Base was twenty minutes from Seattle-Tacoma International Airport. The FBI had requested that the parachutes be sent from McChord. If his demands were not met, he would detonate the bomb and kill everyone on board. The other passengers remained totally oblivious to the circumstances surrounding them.

Seattle lawyer Larry Finegold, an assistant U.S. Attorney at the time, was one of the thirty-six passengers on Flight 305. Finegold stated that he did not suspect anything unlawful. "I did not suspect a skyjacking or other criminal conduct while we were in the air. However, given that we were circling Seattle for an hour or two while the pilot was telling us he was in touch with the ground, I did suspect that the plane was in trouble due to weather or mechanical difficulties." Finegold learned the truth when he left the plane and recognized an FBI agent, whom he knew, standing on the tarmac. At that point, he was told the plane had been hijacked.

The plane circled over Sea-Tac for about three hours, until FBI officials radioed the crew that they had the money and parachutes. At 5:45 p.m. Flight 305 landed at Sea-Tac. All on board except for the flight crew—two pilots, a flight engineer, and a flight attendant—were allowed to leave the airplane. The flight attendant who had initially communicated with the skyjacker disembarked, and a second stewardess took the seat next to him and relayed his demands forward via the plane's intercom. As the jet was refueled, a courier brought the ransom to the 727. Cooper received 10,000 unmarked twenty-dollar bills from Northwest Orient Airlines, as requested, but before the plane landed in Seattle, FBI agents copied every bill, making a permanent record of the serial numbers.

After receiving the $200,000 and four parachutes, the hijacker next asked to be flown to Mexico. He also demanded that the plane fly at not more than 200 miles an hour and at an altitude of 10,000 feet with its landing gear down and wing flaps lowered to fifteen degrees. The pilots informed Cooper that even with full fuel tanks, the 727 would not make it to Mexico flying at low speed with its landing gear and flaps down. They convinced the man that the plane would have to land in Reno, Nevada, to refuel.

At 7:40 p.m. the 727 left the runway at Sea-Tac. After asking the flight attendant for instructions on lowering the stairway at the back of the plane, Cooper ordered her into the cockpit where he told her to stay until the plane landed. Before closing the first class compartment's curtain, she glanced back just long enough to see Cooper tying something around his waist.

A blinking red light on the instrument panel caught the pilots' attention a little before 8 p.m. The light indicated one of the airplane's doors was ajar. The flight crew guessed that Cooper had opened the passenger staircase in the plane's tail section. About eleven minutes later the crew felt pressure changes in their ears and noticed bumps on their gauges as they flew over the Lewis River near the town of La Center in southwestern Washington. The pilot radioed the ground and reported that they thought their passenger had just left the plane. When the 727 landed in Reno, there was no sign of Cooper, the $200,000, or two of the four parachutes. All that remained were two parachutes, a thin, black tie and pearl tiepin, and a pile of cigarette butts. Cords from one of the remaining parachutes had been removed, probably to tie the money satchel around his waist. FBI agents surmised that Cooper had jumped at 8:11 p.m., when the pressure gauges recorded the bumps, over south Cowlitz or north Clark County, Washington. They believed the bumps were caused by the skyjacker jumping off the stairs and the ramp bouncing up afterwards.

Two jets from McChord Air Force Base were able to follow within five miles of the passenger plane. The Air Force pilots never saw anyone jump from the 727 in the dark, rain-soaked skies over southwestern Washington. One of the parachutes was a sports chute that may have enabled Cooper to jump without being seen. The second was an inoperable training parachute that had mistakenly been included with the others.

The story of the hijacking was soon broadcast and printed across the nation. The press learned that the FBI was interested in a Portland resident. When it was reported that a Portland man with the initials D. B. Cooper was a person of interest, the hijacker became identified thereafter as D. B. Cooper even after Portland's Cooper had been cleared. The actual hijacker never referred to himself as anyone but Dan Cooper.

FBI agents, local authorities, and more than 300 Fort Lewis soldiers scoured the southwestern corner of the state for eighteen days with no success. The rugged, wooded terrain was examined by air, by river and on foot, but not a trace of the mysterious Dan Cooper was to be found until Brian Ingram discovered the tattered bills nine years later. Since the loot was found under such a thin layer of sediment, geologists who studied the site concluded that it had been swept to the location by a stream within a year or two of the find. After Ingram's discovery FBI agents found a few more dirty fragments of bills and some broken rubber bands. Seattle FBI agent Jack Pringle said of the search, "We'll work today and tomorrow and probably knock it off and bring my troops back up here and reassess the situation. Some of the area is inaccessible and there's no way we can search the whole river." The hunt was called off on February 15, 1980, after fresh snowfall had covered the ground. None of the ransom money has ever turned up in circulation. Nor has a body or even a scrap of clothing been found. The eruption of Mount St. Helens on May 18, 1980, and ensuing mudflows may have buried any existing evidence forever.

Who was Dan Cooper? He was a man who showed familiarity with the Northwest and had probably spent time near Tacoma, possibly during military service. He was an experienced parachutist, again pointing to the likelihood of military experience. Under the heading, "Cooper Is No 'Robin Hood,'" the January 1972 Air Line Pilots Association's *Pilot Bulletin* told its members, "He demonstrated more than passing knowledge of the air environment, especially parachuting. It is possible that 'D. B. Cooper's' path may have crossed that of airline personnel—and airline pilots—at some time under another name. He is reported to have a bitter hatred against the airlines—he may have worked for one. For these reasons *Pilot Bulletin* is printing the specifications of the criminal that extorted $200,000 from Northwest Airlines on Nov. 24, 1971." The FBI sketch and description of the skyjacker followed.

Several suspects materialized during the investigation, one very dramatically when on April 7, 1972, a Utah man named Richard Floyd McCoy Jr. parachuted out the rear exit of a United Airlines 727 on a flight from Denver to Los Angeles with $500,000 strapped to his body. The hijacker was arrested and sentenced to forty-five years in a federal penitentiary. The elusive McCoy escaped from custody and was killed in 1974 in a gunfight when the FBI attempted to re-arrest him. McCoy was an experienced pilot, Green Beret and Vietnam veteran. During the hijacking the Cooper look-alike handed the flight attendant a note saying that he had a bomb and warning, "No funny stuff."

After this and several other "copy-cat" hijackings, the Federal Aviation Administration made it mandatory to install on all Boeing 727s a device that would keep the rear stair door locked from the outside while the planes were in flight. This apparatus became known as a Cooper Vane. In 1972 scanning of all carry-on baggage was mandated at airports across the country. This did not stop a would-be Seattle hijacker eight years later from telling the crew that he had a bomb and wanted $100,000 and two parachutes. A clever flight attendant drugged the Cooper wannabe with two Valiums, after which he let the Portland-bound passengers leave the plane, changed his ransom to a request for a rental car and three cheeseburgers, and then gave up.

Over the years many more persons of interest emerged. An untold number of ex-husbands and boyfriends' names were given to authorities. A man who killed his mother, wife, and three children several weeks before the skyjacking in 1971 and then disappeared for eighteen years emerged as a suspect after he was caught

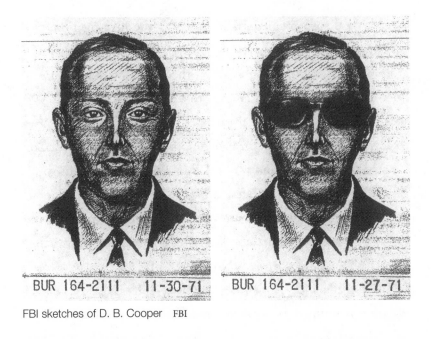

BUR 164-2111   11-30-71   BUR 164-2111   11-27-71

FBI sketches of D. B. Cooper   FBI

and brought to trial in New Jersey in 1990. The suspect, John List, was ruled out later when investigations showed that he was most likely in Denver when the hijacking occurred.

On his deathbed in 1995, a Florida man, Duane Weber, told his wife, Jo, that he was Dan Cooper. Jo had learned after she married Duane in 1977 that he had served a prison sentence at McNeil Island Federal Penitentiary in Puget Sound near Tacoma. She had several odd conversations with her husband over the years. He said he had once hurt his knee "jumping out of an airplane" and told her that common road flares could be put together with clay to resemble a bomb. On a visit to Washington in 1979, Duane pointed to an old logging road north of the Columbia River and stated, "That's where D. B. Cooper walked out of the woods." Then, in 1994, Jo found an aged plane ticket from Portland to Seattle among her husband's things. The FBI has interviewed Mrs. Weber, reviewed Duane's papers and possessions, and—as recently as 2003—asked for any objects that might still contain Weber's DNA.

In late 1988, at a press conference at the Red Lion Inn in Bellevue, Washington, forensic experts were to examine a dirty scrap of nylon cloth that had some strings hanging off of it. The suspicious fabric had been found in the Columbia River and it was hoped it could be linked to Dan Cooper. To everyone's disappointment, the hanky-sized, white-nylon cloth was determined not to be from a piece of Cooper's parachute.

Following the death of Nebraskan Elsie Rodgers in 2000, her family provided the FBI with a skull that she had kept in a box. She had told her family that she found it in southwestern Washington near the Columbia River in the early 1980s and thought it was Cooper's. At the time she had tried to turn the skull over to authorities, but when nobody would listen to her, she took it home with her to Nebraska. FBI agents tested the skull, comparing DNA to that Cooper had left behind on his cigarettes, but could not link the two.

Whoever he was, D. B. Cooper became a folk hero—a man who pulled off the only unsolved skyjacking in United States history with what the FBI now believes was a briefcase full of wires and road flares. The hijacker who jumped from an airplane into a raging storm with twenty-one pounds of twenty-dollar bills strapped to his body has been immortalized in books, movies, and songs. After the incident some Northwesterners were fond of wearing T-shirts printed with the saying, "D. B. Cooper, Where Are You?"

The FBI spent more money investigating the hijacking than Cooper was paid, scrutinizing as many as 10,000 suspects. IRS agents calculate Cooper's tax bill with penalties at well over $200,000. Globe Indemnity Company, the insurance agency that paid the claim, would probably sue him to recover the funds. Federal law provides for a five-year statute of limitations on Aircraft Piracy; however, U.S. Code and case law also state, "No statute of limitations shall extend to any person fleeing from justice." With no statute of limitations on his act of air piracy and escape from justice, Cooper could still be sent to prison were he ever to be found.

FBI agent Ralph Himmelsbach, an investigator on the case until 1980 when he retired, gave the opinion that Cooper "was very likely an ex-con who was going to make one last, desperate go for the big one. If he made it, fine. If not, he probably felt he had very little to lose." Himmelsbach believed that Cooper died in the wilds of southwestern Washington, probably near Lake Merwin, after jumping from the airplane. Cooper had dived into freezing rain and subzero temperatures. Fierce winds would have immediately blown the loafers off his feet. Still, the retired investigator was willing to admit, "We have to accept the possibility that we may never know. I guess we can live with that, if we have to." Ingram's discovery was made just two weeks before the Portland agent retired. Of that he told the press, "It's ironic isn't it? The first and only concrete bit of information comes only 17 days before I retire."

For his part in the investigation, Ingram got a $2,760 reward. Three hundred dollars of the reward consisted of fifteen of the original twenty-dollar bills paid Cooper as a ransom. Ingram bought a VCR and a motorcycle for himself. The balance went into a college fund at a local bank.

In August 2011, the FBI reported that it had received a credible tip from a person in law enforcement. The tip led agents to a woman who claimed that her uncle, L. D. Cooper (who died ten years earlier), was D. B. Cooper. Marla Cooper remembered her uncle appearing at her grandmother's Oregon home on Thanksgiving Day in 1971 "bloody and bruised." He had left the day before to go turkey hunting, and when he returned, claimed he had been in a car accident. That memory, coupled with other family members' comments over the years, convinced Marla that her uncle was D. B. Cooper. Though the FBI called the story "a promising lead," they were not able to lift fingerprints from the items Ms. Cooper provided to match those partial prints the hijacker left behind on a magazine and in the plane's cabin. The FBI later determined that there was no DNA match between the samples the family provided for L. D. Cooper and the trace DNA extracted from the hijacker's tie in 2001. Investigators stated that the partial DNA sample from the tie could be used to exclude a suspect, but not to identify one.

And to this day, the FBI continues to investigate the case of D. B. Cooper.

DEMONS OF THE DEEP

On Saturday, July 1, 1893, a group of seven men set sail from Tacoma on a three-day fishing and hunting trip. The party consisted of five locals—W. Fitzhenry, H. Beal, W. McDonald, J. Bell, H. Blackwood—and two Easterners. Initially they fished off Point Defiance until a shift in the wind motivated them to move their vessel into Black Fish Bay on Henderson Island, where they decided to camp overnight next to a trout stream. A crew of surveyors from Olympia was also camped nearby.

Around midnight the camping men were suddenly awakened by a horrible noise, like the roar of thunder, and a stinging electrical current traveling through the air. One of the Eastern visitors described the sensation: "The whole air was filled with a strong current of electricity that caused every nerve in the body to sting with pain, and a light as bright as that created by the concentration of many arc lights kept constantly flashing."

The fishermen and the surveyors jumped to their feet and stood on the banks of the stream. Turning their attention toward the source of the energy, the men were horrified to see a monster in the bay. As it approached the shore, it expelled from the center of its head a torrent of water that looked to the campers like blue fire. Its oval body was estimated to be 150 feet long and 30 feet around at its thickest part, with copper-colored bands, which seemed to emit electricity, encircling the body every few feet. The head was shaped like the head of an enormous walrus and adorned with a crop of coarse hair. Two hornlike points jutted from the center of its head. A rotating, propeller-like tail guided its movements.

One of the men from the surveyors' camp walked toward the water for a better look. As he did so, the monster darted toward the shore and spewed a stream of water at the man, knocking him to the ground where he lay as if dead. When McDonald attempted to aid the downed surveyor, he too was struck by water the monster was expelling and fell to the sand unconscious. The others ran for the woods leaving their fallen comrades on the beach below. From their hiding place they could see that when the serpent dived below the surface, it left a luminous trail in its wake. It took the men some time to work their way back to the beach in total darkness. They were relieved to find their two friends alive, though still unconscious. By daylight the two men had been revived. The campers were so convinced they had seen a real sea monster that at dawn they broke camp and sailed for Tacoma. One of the sportsmen from the East reported his intent to send a full account of the encounter to The Smithsonian Institution, as he was sure they would send some "scientific chaps" out to investigate.

———

Sightings of sea serpents in the Pacific Northwest have been reported for hundreds of years, starting with Northwest tribes. The Squamish believed that the sea serpent or Salt Chuck Oluk was evil. The monster was sighted more frequently during the gold rush to the Fraser River in the mid-1800s. Tribal members guiding the prospectors north reported the white men's great greed and love for gold were causing starvation, murder, and madness among them. Since the Squamish sightings of Salt Chuck Oluk so increased during these times, one chief described the monster as a "hated totem of what now rules the white man's world—greed and love of chickimin (money)."

Ancient native carvings and petroglyphs depicting sea serpents have been discovered in western Washington. The most famous and well-documented of these is the Skagit River Atlatl. Found in the Skagit River Delta near the town of La Conner, the atlatl was carbon dated to 200 AD. The spear launcher, carved from the wood of a yew tree, depicted a ferocious sea serpent.

Non-native witnesses began telling of sea-serpent sightings in and around Puget Sound with greater frequency beginning in the late 1800s. Many sightings have occurred in the Strait of Juan de Fuca between Washington's Olympic Peninsula and Victoria, B.C., on Vancouver Island. The Straits of Haro (running north/south) and Juan de Fuca (east/west) form the border between Canada and the United States at Washington State.

Hildegard B. Forbes, the wife of Dr. Henry S. Forbes, a physician and chairman of the Alaska Committee for the Association on American Indian Affairs, wrote of spotting a sea serpent in August 1912 while she was on board a steamer to Alaska. As the ship passed through the strait system, she witnessed a dark-colored, snakelike creature about 40 feet long, swimming southward. The head, with its seaweedlike mane, was raised out of the water as it swam. The body had five to seven humps that rose and fell as it moved along.

A lawyer and clerk with the British Columbia Legislature, Major W. H. Langley, reported seeing a sea serpent on Sunday, October 1, 1933, while he was sailing along Haro Strait between San Juan Island and Victoria. Noises—a loud gruntlike snort and hissing—made by the animal first attracted the attention of the major and his wife. The major told the *Victoria Daily Times* that the creature was as big as a large whale but entirely different: "Its color was very distinct as the sun was shining brightly on its wetted surface and it was such a short distance away . . . Its color was of a greenish brown . . . sort of dark olive green. It had markings along the top and sides. It seemed to be of a serrated nature . . . The only part of it that we saw was a huge dome of what was apparently a portion of its back."

After learning of Langley's story, F.W. Kemp, a British Columbia Provincial Archives officer, admitted that he and his family had witnessed such a being in the same vicinity the summer before, on August 10, 1932. Mrs. Kemp was sitting on the beach when a commotion in the water threw a wash against the shore like the wake of a powerboat. Mr. Kemp and his son then noticed an enormous denizen of the deep. He described a huge creature traveling with its head raised above the water. Near a steep bluff, the serpent slid 10 feet of its head and body onto a rock and commenced to rub itself against the rough surface. The movements were like those of a crocodile. They were able to see the entire length of the creature that lay above the water line. The Kemps could plainly see its serrated back, which resembled the cutting edge of a saw near the tail. The animal's head was oval and its body, a glistening greenish brown. Around the head appeared a sort of mane, which drifted round the body like kelp. After several minutes the sea monster slid off the rock and swam away from them, thrashing the water into lather with its tail. The family estimated the size of the serpent at 80 feet gauged by the size of logs on the beach.

So many came forward after these reports were published that editor Archie Wills of the *Victoria Daily Times* held a contest to name the sea serpent. The winning entry was "Cadborosaurus," or "Caddy" for short, named for the Cadboro Bay just north of Victoria where it had been seen. Even after limiting reports to those that were signed and verified, Wills compiled a list of around 100 people, including three sea captains and the pilot who flew the mail between Seattle and Victoria, who had seen the beast.

Documented sightings have occurred at the mouth of the Columbia River and south into Oregon as well. Reporters for *The Oregonian* dubbed the creature Colossal Claude. Sailors reportedly saw Claude on a fairly regular basis in the 1930s. In 1934 the first mate on a Columbia River light ship described a 40-foot-long being that he had seen at the mouth of the river in the Pacific: "It had a neck some eight-feet long, a big round body, a mean-looking tail and an evil, snaky look to its head." Three years later in the same area Captain Charles Graham of the fishing troller *Viv* talked of seeing "a long, hairy, tan-colored creature, with the head of an overgrown horse, about forty-feet long, and with a four-foot waist measure." The crew from a halibut fishing ship working near the entrance to the Columbia River in 1939 all witnessed a sea serpent lift 10 feet of its neck above the ocean and look directly at the startled men.

A student from the University of Washington, "Rusty" Beetle of Port Angeles, told a reporter that he had seen the serpent several years before the published sightings. He was fishing off Dungeness Spit, a narrow strip of beach that juts off the northern end of the Olympic Peninsula into the Strait of Juan de Fuca, when a sea serpent appeared next to his boat and then proceeded to swim around the boat for almost ten minutes. Beetle described a 40-foot-long, serpentlike body that had a head like something between a horse and a camel with a mane. When he returned the boat to its owner in Port Angeles and told of his adventure, the boat owner advised the young UW student not to take a bottle with him when he fished by himself.

Struck by the strange sensation that something was watching him, George Saggers, who was salmon fishing in the Pacific Ocean, felt a shiver run the length of his spine. Turning to the port side of his boat, he saw a head and neck raised up 4 feet from the water. Two protruding black eyes, 3 inches in diameter, were staring directly at the shocked fisherman. Saggers described the creature as "a mottled color of gray and light brown," with a head and neck of the same dimensions—about 18 inches thick. When it lost interest in Saggers, it turned its head away showing him a dark brown mane that ran down its head and neck. His description of the mane was that it "seemed like bundles of warts rather than hair. It looked something like a mattress would, if split down the middle allowing rolls of cotton batting to protrude." The experienced fisherman concluded that the sea monster appeared unreal and was unlike anything that he had ever seen before.

Judge James T. Brown and his family got a good look at the creature in 1950, as it frolicked in Haro Strait. Mrs. Brown saw the animal rise up out of the water and shouted to her husband

and daughter to look. The head had disappeared by then, but resurfaced 150 yards from the shore. A snakelike head rose 5 feet straight up from the water. About 6 feet behind the head, a dark-colored, vertical coil, a foot wide and about 7 feet long, showed above the water line. The size of the coil gave the judge the feeling that there was "a great length of him under the water." After looking at the family for a moment, it dived and resurfaced 300 yards out just a short time later. The three people saw the thing at the surface three times. Once it came up directly in front of them, giving the judge the image of a serpent, "I'd think the creature was 35 to 40 feet long. It was like a monstrous snake," he said.

Though he has been seen in the open ocean, Caddy seems to prefer the protection of Puget Sound and the Straits of Haro, Georgia and Juan de Fuca. Once again on the Washington side of the Strait of Juan de Fuca, along Dungeness Spit, the serpent materialized for two women and their young sons in March 1953. [Other reports date this sighting to 1961.] Because one of the women, Mrs. Stout, had studied marine biology, her description added credence to the stories of the mythical beast. She described the encounter in a letter to Paul H. LeBlond of the Oceanography Institute for the University of British Columbia.

While watching a freighter travel toward Port Townsend, the women and boys saw what they thought was a tree limb bobbing in the water. After disappearing below the water line, the thing resurfaced much closer to the beachcombers this time. One of the little boys began to cry and cling to his mother. The creature's large, flattish head was turned, looking at the ship, and three humps appeared below an elongated neck. After submerging again, the being came up even closer to them than before. All viewers could now see a pattern of burnt orange markings against a darker brown skin. The neck sticking above the ocean was about 6 feet long; behind that the humps of the body were estimated at a height of 5 feet apiece. The 20-inch head and long neck were topped with a long, floppy mane. Except for the humps, it resembled pictures of herbivorous marsh-living dinosaurs. As the group watched, the creature sank and rose in a nearly perpendicular manner, moved its neck to and fro, and swiveled its head around. As a biologist, Mrs. Stout found the sight of the creature difficult to accept, yet all of the members of the little group had observed the animal for about eight minutes.

In April 1958 a group including a minister from the Mount Vernon Presbyterian Church saw a sea serpent at least 12 feet long off the shore of Whidbey Island. They watched as the creature swam along undulating as it moved through the water.

Two fishermen gave chase to a serpent one-half mile from the Discover Island Lighthouse in the Strait of Juan de Fuca in 1959. One of the men spotted the thing about 80 feet in front of their boat. As it began to move away from them they decided to chase it. When the curious fishermen were within 30 feet of the creature, it submerged, dropping straight down into the sea. Arriving at the spot where it had gone down, all they could see was turbulent water. The creature traveled at such great speed that it surfaced 100 yards from the boat just a few moments later. David Miller, one of the fishermen, wrote in a letter to oceanographer Paul LeBlond that, with all of the marine life that he had seen over his many years at sea, nothing he had ever seen remotely resembled this thing. Both men marveled at the creature's huge, reddish eyes

and short ears. Miller said in his letter that his brother had also seen the same creature on a later occasion.

Similarities between witnesses' accounts of the oval, long-necked creature's appearance and demeanor cannot be dismissed. Most seem to agree on the dark, greenish brown color. The Tacoma sea monster was described as having copper bands, while the Dungeness Spit creature had bright, burnt orange reticulations. While Mr. and Mrs. Kemp described the animal sliding its head and body onto a rock, the Squamish told legends of a gigantic sea serpent stretched across the surface of the waters—its head resting on a group of rocks below a bluff. Almost all sightings involve a marine animal that can raise a great length of its neck out of the water.

Sea monster carcass discovered in 1934 on Henry Island, San Juan County, Washington *The Illustrated London News Picture Library*

There is little doubt that witnesses have seen a real, possibly mammalian, sea creature. Noted Belgian zoologist Bernard Heuvelmans designated the study of such unknowns as cryptozoology and the "hidden animals" as cryptids. Heuvelmans was known as the Father of Cryptozoology, and his research included sea serpents known as marine cryptids. Heuvelmans investigated well over 500 reported sightings throughout the oceans of the world. The sightings he discovered ranged in time from the seventeenth century through the twentieth century. He thoroughly researched each account, accepting only sightings that could be scientifically proven. Heuvelmans documented seven types of sea serpents: long-necked, merhorse, many-humped, many-finned, super-otter, super-eel and marine saurian. Though witness's descriptions of

Washington's sea monsters vary, most seem to fit Heuvelmans's merhorse category, including characteristic long necks, horselike heads, big eyes, whiskers, and manes.

There are many theories about what these marine cryptids might actually be. Some suggest that the sea serpents are really giant conger eels swimming on their sides, thus creating the illusion of vertical undulation. These eels have also been known sometimes to swim with their heads above water. Large colonies of jellyfish or other sea-going invertebrates can be massive in length, and appear to undulate and spew forth seawater. Could it be a gigantic oarfish, usually an inhabitant of the deepest ocean floors?

Remains of purported sea serpents have been thought by fisheries experts to be the bodies of giant oarfish, sometimes called ribbonfish. A fisherman hauling in his nets in 1944 found the body of a gigantic, serpentlike creature on a Vancouver Island shore. The head was like that of a sheep and the spinal column about 40 feet long with a dorsal fin the length of its body. Fisheries experts initially classified the animal as a ribbonfish. Oarfish or ribbonfish have elongated serpentine bodies with long pelvic fins, and dorsal fins running from head to tail. These strange fish can grow to 60 feet in length and are rarely seen on the ocean's surface.

In 1934 a 30-foot-long creature with a horselike head and the remnants of four large fins washed up on one of Washington's San Juan Islands, Henry Island. Divers know Henry Island for its fascinating sea caves, which house sizeable sea creatures. Witnesses who saw the carcass on the beach said it had reddish skin and was covered with hair and quills. It was taken to the nearest research facility at the British Columbia Government Biological Station where the remains were judged to be those of a basking shark. Still, the curators at Victoria's Provincial Museum declared the corpse that of the last remaining Steller's sea cow. The sea cow, a huge manatee-like aquatic mammal, was discovered in 1741 in the Bering Sea. The enormous creatures, known to grow to 20 to 30 feet in length, were thought to have been hunted to extinction before 1800. Heuvelmans concluded the Henry Island creature was indeed a basking shark. As the body of the gigantic shark disintegrates, the head takes on the look of a plesiosaur's, or is sometimes described as being like a horse or camel's head. The rotting skin fibers take on the appearance of whiskers.

Is the Northwest's sea monster some yet-to-be discovered marine life or a holdover from the dinosaur era thought to be extinct? No explanation will ever satisfy all true believers in sea serpents; and, as one of the witnesses to Tacoma's sea monster exclaimed, "There are denizens of the ocean that man never in his most horrible and fantastic nightmare even saw the likes of."

LEGEND OF THE TWO
SADDLES TREASURE

A tired, dirty, bedraggled little family reached the small community of Trinidad along the Columbia River after a long but uneventful journey south from Canada. John Welch, his wife, and daughter, Anna, along with two other men and an Indian guide, had been prospecting in British Columbia for five months. The difficult life and backbreaking work of mining in Fraser River country had paid off for the Welch family. John had mined over $85,000 in gold dust and nuggets when he decided to return his family to their home in Portland, Oregon.

Unfortunately for the Welches the trip through central Washington would not go as smoothly as the first half of the trek had gone.

Angry at the influx of miners in the Columbia Basin, some of the members of the plateau tribes of the Mid-Columbia Region were becoming increasingly hostile to prospectors in 1876. Chief Moses of the Columbia tribe was the leader and spokesman for the bands of the Mid-Columbia Plateau. Although the government had attempted to force Chief Moses and his Columbia people onto the Yakama Reservation, he was dissatisfied with the subpar arrangement. Emboldened by his cousin, Chief Joseph, and his war, which was then in progress, the chief set up a large camp near Moses Coulee, which grew when the Columbia tribe was joined by the Wenatchee, Okanogan, Methow, Chelan, and up to half a dozen other plateau tribes. As the size of the gathering grew, settlers in the area became increasingly nervous. When the Welch party reached the Trinidad Bar area, they learned that Chief Moses and his men had been threatening and chasing off the Chinese who had been panning for gold on the Columbia. Some thought the Chinese were responsible for the death of Chief Moses' brother. During one incident in 1875, 300 Chinese gold panners working on a plateau hundreds of feet above the river were surrounded by a group of plateau Indians. Backed up against the cliffs high above the Columbia with nowhere to go, the entire group of placer miners was killed, their bodies thrown over the cliffs into the river below.

In light of the Indians' prevailing attitudes toward miners in the Columbia Basin, the party's guide suggested they bury their gold and valuables and lay low for a while until the hostilities died down. Their Indian guide also told them to turn their horses loose and continue the trek on foot. With that advice, the guide told Welch and company that they were on their own, and he disappeared permanently.

After dark, Welch loaded two packhorses with supplies and his precious cargo and rode away from camp. He found a place on the steep basalt cliff walls along the Columbia River's east bank approximately 8 miles south of the town of Quincy to secure his cache. There he dug a hole and buried two saddles, his daughter Anna's hairbrush, comb, ribbons, a rosewood box containing personal papers, and a few other personal effects. He built a stone monument over the cache to mark the spot. From the pile of rocks, Welch walked to another secure location and buried his pokes and parcels of gold nuggets. Before he left his treasure, he drew a map of the area and its landmarks. Not long after Welch returned to his group, their camp was discovered by a war party who held them under attack for days.

Welch's family and partners hid out in a canyon for three days while the hostilities continued along the river gorge. Under cover of darkness the men took turns sneaking from the shelter of their camp near the cliff walls of the river to a stream to get drinking water. The assault ended after three days of fighting. Feeling it was safe to leave the area, the group packed up and moved out. They had not gone very far when a party of Columbias on horseback stopped them. Terrified, the Welch party was held hostage to the whims of the men who outnumbered them. The riders searched through their packs and equipment and took a few items that interested them. Then, to everyone's surprise they let the Welch party go on its way. Perhaps the fact that they had no gold with them convinced the Indians that they were not stealing the precious metal from their lands. Furthermore, groups traveling with women and children were not considered as threatening as groups of armed men were perceived to be.

As soon as Welch got to Fort Vancouver, he asked for an armed military escort to accompany him back to Inland Columbia River country to recover his possessions, including the gold. Fort Vancouver's commanding officer denied the request because his men were needed elsewhere. Welch and his men thought better of returning to the river by themselves. As late as 1879 the Army

Columbia River Gorge at Babcock Bench area near Quincy
ALAN BAUER PHOTOGRAPHY

was still trying to relocate the plateau tribes onto reservations. Washington Territorial Governor Elisha P. Ferry wrote to the U.S. secretary of the interior that a feeling of insecurity prevailed among the settlers of eastern Washington, who were surrounded by "disaffected and discontented Indians, who might at any moment and with little warning, commence hostilities." Even after Governor Ferry and the Army reached a resolution ensuring peace with the inland tribes at a council near Wenatchee, broken agreements caused incidents with angry individual Indians to continue well into the 1880s.

The Welch family resumed their lives in Oregon's Willamette Valley. For the next twenty-seven years, no one from the

Welch expedition made any attempt to recover the buried gold. By 1903 John Welch had decided to search the Columbia River area for his cache of gold. When he arrived in central Washington he found the terrain unfamiliar and drastically changed over the nearly thirty years since he had been there. He returned home to Portland empty handed, but planned to go back the next summer and hire a local guide who was familiar with the area.

In 1904 Welch and a friend made the trek north in search of his buried treasure. When they arrived at the town of Trinidad, they registered at the local hotel and asked about procuring a guide who knew the territory well. Mr. Van Slyke, the manager of the Trinidad Hotel, recommended his fourteen-year-old son, saying he knew the area better than anybody else. Young L. H. Van Slyke noted that Welch and his partner were prepared to do quite a bit of riding during the excursion. Welch had brought his own well-padded saddle with him from Portland.

The boy was asked to help Welch locate a cave in the high basalt bluffs overlooking the Columbia River. This particular cave would have a stream flowing nearby. Young Van Slyke was told that the Welch family had been attacked by a war party years ago and had buried their possessions. Welch had the youth take him to a sizeable box canyon in the Ancient Lake area, near the town of Quincy. Though the three riders combed the entire area on horseback for weeks, they failed to find any sign of Welch's cache. Nothing looked familiar to Welch, so with great regret he eventually had to call off the search.

When he felt he was too old to return to the box canyon, he gave the treasure map to his daughter, Anna E. Tuttle of Portland.

She told no one of the family secret. For six summers beginning around 1909, she traveled to Trinidad and spent four to six weeks scouring the Columbia canyons for her father's treasure. She hunted for the pile of rocks that marked the grave of the two saddles, digging through sand, rocks, caves, and potholes along the river bank. She knew that if she could locate the saddles and personal effects, the gold would not be far off. Cowboys hired to guide her over the years reported that Tuttle had told them, "Show me where the saddles are buried and I can walk to the gold."

For six years Tuttle picked through rocks, dug up sand, scoured caves and potholes, and each year came up with nothing. Every year as townsfolk heard of her return, they would form search parties to help look for the gold. As the years passed, though, townspeople began to make fun of Anna Welch Tuttle's treasure hunts and to ridicule anyone who assisted her in the endeavors. After a sixth fruitless search expedition, Tuttle returned to Portland for the last time. With no trace of the two saddles ever located, she had decided to give her search up permanently. Anna Welch Tuttle passed away in Portland in 1929.

About six years after Tuttle's last search, two trappers, Ted Williams and Harry "Bud" Webley, were trapping along the basalt bluffs above the Columbia about 200 feet above the water-line, when they found a coyote caught in one of their snares. Upon examining their trap, the men noticed a piece of worn leather strap sticking out of the dirt at the mouth of a cave halfway up the steep cliff. While attempting to dig itself free, the wild coyote had dug a hole through the floor of the cave and uncovered part of an old buried saddle. Webley and Williams, being locals, were familiar with the legend of the two saddles gold, but they had never thought of it as much more than a folktale. The trappers dug beneath the sand and rock and found one worn saddle, and then a second old saddle. Digging further, they uncovered a rosewood box containing personal documents, a child's hairbrush, ribbons, a long-stemmed pipe, a pair of old-fashioned glasses, two bells used to stake out horses, and a few other personal effects. They remembered the old story and realized that this was the cache of old man Welch's that Anna Tuttle had been seeking for so many years. Williams told a reporter for the *Wenatchee Daily World*, "Webley and I had heard much about Mrs. Tuttle and her explorations in search of the buried gold, but we never took any stock in the proposition until we set a trap for a coyote in a cave that had been hollowed out of the rock in a pothole about a mile from the river near Smyrna, and thus uncovered the caches of hidden articles."

Next, the trappers began hunting for the treasure that, according to legend, was to be found within walking distance of the rock cairn. Williams said, "We talked with cowboys who had acted as guides for her, also with Mrs. Sarah Truax, who formerly lived nearby but has moved to Ellensburg, also other neighbors who remembered parts of her story. This convinced me that there must be something to the tradition, and so I have spent some time digging around in the vicinity to see if I could discover the gold also." They spent months searching, but came up empty.

Since they couldn't find the gold, the two men decided to tell Anna Tuttle what they had discovered. Unfortunately, the Trinidad Hotel had burned down. The fire had also consumed all records and guest registers, which contained the names of

Tuttle or her family. Hotel manager Van Slyke had moved with his family to Olympia after the fire. One of the cowboys who had guided Tuttle on her last trip told Williams that she had actually been very close to the site where the saddles were discovered. On that last expedition she had stood on the rocks just above the cave where the discovery was later made. At that time she said that she believed that was the place her father had stood to scope out a safe burial spot to hide his gold. Tuttle and her guide thoroughly dug up the area, but found nothing. The Wenatchee paper quoted Ted Williams, "I feel sure, however, that if we can find Mrs. Tuttle and take her to the cave where we found the saddles, she will remember where the gold is buried." When someone told Williams they thought that Anna Tuttle might be living in Salem, he traveled to Oregon looking for her, but did not find her at the address provided him. The trapper was able to find an old man at the county poor farm who had once financed one of Mrs. Tuttle's gold-hunting excursions with a loan of $1,000. The resourceful Williams discovered that the lost gold had been reported to the United States Mint, and that the Seattle branch of the mint still had a record of the missing gold. Welch would have registered the loss to establish ownership of his cache, in case another party ever claimed it. Ted Williams and Bud Webley gave up searching for the Welch family descendants as well as the treasure.

Floodwaters that backed up behind the newly constructed Wanapum Dam covered much of the area in 1963. The Wanapum Dam flood renewed interest in the buried John Welch treasure. In 1964, L. H. Van Slyke, John Welch's young guide on the 1904 treasure hunt, gave an interview to a local newspaper in which he stated that he did not believe that rising water had covered up the Welch treasure. The impression that Welch had given him during the search was that the gold was buried on a high point that overlooked the Columbia River. If it still exists today the site would be near the family's hideout on a basalt bluff, in a box canyon with a spring flowing through the rocks nearby.

THE GEORGETOWN CASTLE

When Ray McWade, a Seattle artist and gallery owner, was offered the Queen Anne Victorian for $16,000, he decided to gamble on the rundown, rambling, turreted old Georgetown mansion. The once elegant turn-of-the-century home had been vacant for years, except for transients who lit fires on the hardwood floors to keep warm. One such fire had burned a hole from the bottom floor, clear through the roof. Still, Ray decided to take a chance on living in and restoring the home to its former beauty.

Though he initially moved in alone, when Ray's friend, Petter Pettersen, who had recently moved to Seattle, needed a place to stay, Ray extended an offer to share the new home. Petter moved there in late 1973, or early 1974, shortly after Ray purchased it. When the men moved into the house, only one small room on the ground floor was habitable; and though the house had nine bedrooms and three bathrooms, the only working bathroom was on the second floor. His first night in the house, Petter was preparing for bed and ascended the stairs to the second floor bathroom. As he reached the top of the staircase, chills shot up and down his spine, every hair on his body stood on end, and he was overcome by an intense fear. "I have never had such a feeling in my life," remembered Petter. He grabbed a hammer, which was lying nearby, for protection and continued upstairs.

Petter said nothing of the incident when he returned downstairs. Unaware, Ray went up to take his shower. While descending the stairs he suddenly felt a push from behind. Since part of the handrail was missing, he placed his hands along the wall and inched his way downstairs. When he related this event to his roommate, Petter confessed his own experience that he had previously been too embarrassed to tell Ray.

Back in the only livable bedroom, the roommates were watching Johnny Carson on TV when a coat that Ray had hung on the closet door began to move. The silhouette of the garment at first seemed far away and then it began moving toward them. They both stared, as the coat seemed to come alive. A face materialized in the folds of the fabric, followed by the figure of an older woman with a "Katharine Hepburn-type hairdo." The woman's left hand clutched her throat, and she appeared to be gasping for air. In her right hand she held a handkerchief. Over her right shoulder an ornate picture frame containing a portrait of a man floated in midair. He had a swarthy complexion and black, lacquered-down hair that was parted in the middle. The ghostly visitor began striking toward Ray's bed with the handkerchief. The astonished witnesses watched the apparition for several seconds until Ray exclaimed, "Her name is Sarah." The instant the name was spoken, the woman disappeared. Ray felt that she had not only been providing her identity, but that she had been trying to explain how she had died.

Feeling quite shaken by the experience, Ray decided to leave the room, so he headed in the direction of the kitchen. In order to get there he had to go through two doorways of a small,

Georgetown Castle, 1935   Washington State Archives, Puget Sound Regional Branch, King County Real Property Record Collection

nonworking bathroom. After Ray passed through the first doorway, his body was bounced backward from the second opening when he tried to pass through it. Petter witnessed this happen twice; both times Ray was clutching at his own throat and gasping for breath. The third time, Petter and Ray grabbed hold of each other's hands for support and made it through the doorframe together. Though they had broken through some sort of force, they both felt an evil presence had been released. Ray felt the evil came from the dark, Mediterranean-type man he had seen depicted in the portrait. He believed the dark-skinned man had been killed in the turret on the third floor of the house. Ray sensed the man might have been Sarah's husband, but found out later that she had not been married.

The mansion's occupants saw Sarah many times after their initial encounter. They would open the front door to enter the home, and she would be there for a split second. Odd things occurred during the weeks following Sarah's introduction. One morning Petter opened the front door to find the body of a black cat on the steps. He threw the dead cat into the trash, but the next morning the same cat's corpse was back on the front steps.

Ray opened an art gallery in the Metropole Building in Seattle's Pioneer Square. One evening Petter and Ray had closed up the Pioneer Square gallery and returned home. Ray was just turning his key in the lock when they heard the faint sound of breaking glass off in the distance. Petter went around to the back of the house, and Ray went inside to investigate the damage intruders might have done. Ray found a small window at the back of the house had been broken. There was no glass inside on the windowsill or the floor, as there would be if someone had thrown a rock through the window or tried to break in from the outside. Glass was scattered about on the ground outside of the home as if someone had punched it out from the inside. At that moment Ray remembered that the day before he had inspected that window and considered replacing the clear pane with stained glass. Thinking aloud, he said to Petter, "It looks like Sarah is working too." Then, they heard the faint sound of a woman's giggling.

There were several cold spots on the second floor in the upstairs hallway. Stepping into them felt like "stepping into a deep freeze" since they were always several degrees cooler than the rest of the house. The first such cold spot had been discovered by Ray before Petter moved in. While cleaning and remodeling on the second floor hallway, Ray noticed a section of the wall with a strange angle where the hallway seemed a bit wider. He measured around the wall, but could not account for the space. Upon closer inspection he found a fine crack in the plaster in the shape of an archway. Curious, he broke the wall out with a hammer. To his surprise he found a finished room, just 4 by 3 feet in size, which had been totally walled off. As he exited the tiny room, he was hit with a blast of icy cold air. From that time on, there would always be cold air in that spot, which many people, including Petter and a psychic, would experience.

After working for a while at Ray's art gallery, Petter took a job waiting tables and serving cocktails in the restaurant and bar at the Roosevelt Hotel. Since he worked downtown until the bar closed, Petter did not usually arrive home until after 2 a.m. One such night, he came home to find Ray painting. Petter instantly recognized the visage of the severe-featured, stern-looking woman and exclaimed, "You're painting Sarah." Ray explained that Sarah had come to him while he was painting and had asked him to paint her portrait. She also requested that the finished picture be hung at the top of the stairs, and Ray obliged her request. After the painting was hung, Sarah's presence went from menacing to friendly. Their fear of her disappeared, and they came to believe that she was watching out for them. Often they would see Sarah standing next to her portrait as they came in the front door.

Sarah's spirit became playful and even flirtatious. Sometimes while showering, Ray would find the curtain suddenly wrapped around him. Then, he would catch a shadow in the room from the corner of his eye and hear a soft giggle.

On two occasions Ray was told that Sarah had projected her image onto him. Once while a couple was visiting from Los Angeles, Ray began telling them the ghost stories at their request. The wife started acting strangely, then put her hand on her chest and uttered, "Oh my gosh, you're Sarah." She then blurted out, "She loves you."

The second projection occurred when Petter, Ray, and an art gallery employee who was also a neighbor were riding to work on a Metro bus. They were facing each other on bench seats running along the sides of the bus. Ray turned to say something to his friends and found them staring at him with odd looks on their faces. Both Petter and the neighbor said that for a moment Ray had appeared to be an old woman. Petter recognized the woman's image as Sarah's. They concluded that Sarah must have wanted to see where Ray went every day when he left the house.

Houseguests also saw the Victorian-attired Sarah. On one occasion a woman from Australia was staying at the house. Neither Petter nor Ray had mentioned Sarah's presence to the visitor. After sleeping over one night in the old home, the woman asked, "Who is the old lady?" She had awakened during the night to see an older woman going through her suitcase. Thinking that the woman in her room was another houseguest and that she seemed a bit off, the Australian lady told her, "It is OK, dear, you can look."

Another time, Petter's uncle came from Norway to visit him. Knowing the uncle would have jet lag, Petter told him to make himself at home and feel free to use the kitchen no matter the time. The Norwegian uncle woke up around 3 a.m. and went to the kitchen to make coffee and a sandwich. Hard as he looked, he could not find the bread. As he stood wondering where it might be, a loaf of bread suddenly came sailing through the air from the pantry. At the same time the house cat leapt up and grabbed the kitchen windowsill with its front paws and hung there waiting to be let in. According to Petter, his poor uncle was thoroughly "freaked" by these experiences.

Sarah's presence was seen and felt by many guests. She seemed to have been greatly disturbed by the renovating that went on when Ray and Petter first moved in. Perhaps she thought her home was being torn down. When she could see that the house was loved and cared for, she seemed to calm down. Ray was more sensitive to her presence and was the only one of the two who received communications from her. She told him that she was the sister-in-law of the home's owner, whose name may have been Peter. "Peter" had abused Sarah, resulting in the birth of a baby. Sarah was driven insane when the abuser killed the newborn. The man then locked his wife's sister away on the second floor of the mansion.

As the ghost stories circulated, people began coming to the house, knocking on the door, and asking to see inside. This practice was becoming quite annoying when one day, while Ray was there alone, he found an elderly lady standing in the front room. When she saw him, she asked if she could come in. He replied sarcastically that it appeared she was already in. The visitor explained that she wanted to see the house because it used to belong to her family. At that Ray became more interested and told her of his experiences with the ghost of Sarah and the story she had conveyed to him. Ray showed the visitor his painting of Sarah, which she said resembled her great-aunt. The woman claimed that Ray's story sounded like the family's whispered secret about her great-aunt. The only difference was that the great-aunt's name was not Sarah, but rather Elizabeth. The family had employed servants, though, and one of them was named Sarah. Ray then concluded that perhaps the ghost had been calling out for her servant, Sarah, rather than giving her name as Sarah when he first met her. Still, they continued to call their ghost Sarah.

From the neighbors the roommates learned more of the house's history. The mansion appeared to have been constructed during the Victorian era of the 1880s and 1890s. The neighbors thought it might have been built that long ago, and that the records might have been destroyed in the great Seattle fire of 1889. The home was built on riverfront property before the Duwamish River was diverted by human hand. Since Georgetown was outside Seattle city limits, gambling, prostitution, and illegal sporting events flourished in the area. The original owner was reputed to be a card dealer, who sponsored boxing matches on a barge anchored on the Duwamish in front of his home.

True mansions have a ballroom, and this mansion had a large ballroom with a fold-down stage. The stage was rumored to have been used for illicit shows when the home was a brothel. Long-time neighbors told of the old house being turned into a boarding house for Boeing workers during World War II. The rooming house was called The Castle Inn, giving birth to the name that remains with the old house. Reportedly when the home was remodeled and the front porch torn up, a baby's skeleton was discovered.

The last time Petter saw or heard any sign of Sarah was in the mid-1980s. They were gathered in the kitchen with guests visiting from Los Angeles who had previously heard the ghost stories. One of them asked eagerly if they might catch a glimpse of Sarah. Petter told the visitors that he doubted they would encounter Sarah, saying, "I haven't seen her in years." At that, every cupboard in the room opened wide, then slammed shut, and water began to run in the sink. Simultaneously the startled guests heard the sound of a woman's laughing coming from the second floor. It was as if Sarah was playing a joke on them, while letting them know that, yes, she was still there! When Ray sold the house in the late 1980s, he left Sarah's painting at the top of the stairs pursuant to her wishes.

In 1990 a man named Tim O'Brian purchased the Georgetown Castle and lived in it for the next seven years. Although he personally never experienced the ghost, his neighbors told enough stories to pique his curiosity. Tim was able to ferret out historical details that mesh amazingly with the stories Ray and Petter heard.

Tim's record review showed that Peter Gessner constructed the home in 1902. Gessner had been a blackjack dealer at The Central Cafe. He moved his gambling operations to his Georgetown home after encountering legal problems in Seattle for allowing minors to gamble. In addition to being a gambling house, the home was also said to have been a brothel at one time.

In a 1997 interview, Tim told a *Post-Intelligencer* reporter that Peter Gessner, at age fifty-two, had married a woman twenty-five years younger, named Lizzie (Elizabeth). The couple had a son, also named Peter. Gessner caught his wife in an affair with one of his employees, Edward Ward, after she became pregnant and terminated the pregnancy. Devastated, Peter Gessner killed himself in July 1903 by drinking carbolic acid in a rear bedroom of the house. Lizzie and Ward were married four months later and moved into the Georgetown house. The Gessners' son, Peter, later married a tall, thin, harsh-looking woman named Sarah. Sarah reportedly also had a child by another man. Her husband threw the baby from an upstairs window and buried it under the porch.

The obituary of Peter J. Gessner contains a similar set of facts, showing that he moved to Seattle from Helena, Montana, around 1888 and quickly became one of Seattle's best-known gamblers. He was in charge of the poker games at the Standard Gambling House and later became owner of the games at The Seattle Bar (known for many years as Pioneer Square's The Central Tavern and more recently The Central Saloon). The *Post-Intelligencer* reported that it had exposed activities that forced police to close Gessner's games.

In 1902, Gessner built a beautiful Queen Anne-style home for his family. Gessner's new house was reportedly the handsomest home in Georgetown, but Mr. and Mrs. Gessner separated before their home had been fully furnished. Gessner moved into the unfurnished home with a servant, while Mrs. Gessner and her three young boys remained on the family farm near Sunnydale with her husband's business partner and general manager of the farm, Edward Ward. In 1903 Mrs. Gessner had undergone a "surgical operation" at Seattle's Providence Hospital and was recovering at the farm with the aid of a Mrs. Riemer. Friends told of Gessner becoming moody and brooding over his domestic discord.

Mrs. Riemer and Edward Ward were in the city on July 29, 1903, and went to visit Gessner in Georgetown about farm matters. They were told by his servant that Gessner was sleeping.

Insistent on seeing Gessner, Mrs. Riemer barged into the bedroom but returned saying she could not wake him. Ward then entered the room and found the gambler dead. A strong smell of carbolic acid permeated the quarters; the dead man's tongue and the roof of his mouth were burned; and in an adjacent room an empty cup was found next to a large bottle of carbolic acid. Gessner was fifty-two when he killed himself. He left behind his widow and three young sons, all under the age of ten.

Neighbors call a vacant lot near the house Sarah's Garden and claim that nothing will grow there. One Georgetown resident told a reporter that while she was visiting the house, a portrait painted by a former owner (Ray's painting) came flying off of the wall. Others say they have seen a woman peeking out from an upstairs window. Many believe the woman they have seen is a prostitute named Mary or Magdelena who was murdered in an upstairs bedroom. It is unclear when this could have happened. Some claim to have heard moaning, screaming, or a struggle taking place, but Ray and Petter experienced none of that.

The unusual history, appearance, and experiences of the Georgetown Castle continue to make it host to one of the Northwest's most intriguing and enduring ghost stories.

Years after he had moved from the house, Petter turned the television on one day to see a Northwest afternoon show filming in the Georgetown Castle. A medium was going through the house with the film crew. What startled Petter the most was that the medium stopped in the same two places in the upstairs hallway where Petter had always felt the extreme cold spots. She claimed those very spots were full of psychic energy.

Though Ray no longer lives in Seattle, the spirit of Sarah seems to have followed him wherever he has gone. He says, "Sarah's face still appears in my painting from time to time."

The Georgetown manor has been owned for over a decade by a mother and son who have lovingly restored the house and gardens to their original grandeur. As much as they love their home, both admit to experiencing eerie sensations, feeling unexplained vibrations, and hearing creepy noises while on the stairs and upper floor.

This chapter is dedicated to the memory of former Georgetown Castle resident Petter Pettersen, 2008.

MOUNTAIN DEVILS ON MOUNT ST. HELENS

Coastal tribes called them Selahtiks sometimes spelled See-ahtic, the Yakamas called them St'iyahama, and the tribes of the Upper Cowlitz River country said Stiyaha or Kwi-kwihai (The Whistler). All describe beings that roamed the Cascade Mountain range, sleeping by day and hunting by night. The giant, hairy creatures were known to carry off horses and people. Indian lore describes them as members of the fierce Selahtik tribe, a band of renegades who looked like giant apes and lived like wild animals in secluded caves high in the Cascade Mountains. Children were taught never to say their name, because if the beasts heard their names, they would come and capture a human from the tribe.

Elkanah Walker, a missionary to the Spokane tribe, described local beliefs in a letter written to the missionary board in April 1840. Walker reported that local tribes believed in a race of giants that inhabited a mountain west of their lands. The giants lived near the top of this mountain, which was covered with perpetual snow. Since they could not see in daylight, they hunted and worked at night. The men were thieves, who came to people's lodges and kidnapped them as they slept. Victims were placed under skins and taken to the creatures' homes without ever being awakened. When humans did awaken, they were lost and disoriented and had no sense of direction, their way home totally unknown. These beings left tracks a foot and a half in length. Possessing great strength, the beasts have been known to carry two to three large logs at one time across their backs. Often they stole salmon from Indian nets during the night and devoured the fish raw. People who were awake when the giants came knew they were near by the overwhelmingly strong stench they gave off. It was not uncommon for the creatures to come at night, give three whistles and then throw stones at the humans' lodges.

Elders of the Colville Tribe tell of an Indian man who was kidnapped by the great, hairy beasts. After living with them in their cedar-bark shelters for one year he was returned to the spot from which he had been taken. A hunting party found their tribesman at the exact site he had last been seen, in a trancelike state. When he recovered from the hypnotic spell, he told of living with the giant beasts who were great hunters and able to scamper up impossibly steep cliffs and shoulder heavy loads of game. They hunted by night, leaving their crude bark shelters and returning at daybreak with their prey. The mammoth beings used signals to communicate, sometimes sounding like hooting owls, and they possessed the power to hypnotize their captives. Tribal Elder Isabel Arcasa once said in an interview, "The reports of the big footprints are nothing new. We Indian people know all about those dark people even if we have never seen them."

Indians would never go anywhere near places the Selahtiks were known to inhabit. If tribal members ever encountered the Selahtiks, they were careful not to offend them, believing that if

Ape Cave is a 2,000-year-old lava tube located near Ape Canyon south of Mount St. Helens.   USDA FOREST SERVICE, 1979. PHOTO BY J. NIELAND.

a man were to harm one of the creatures, they would never forget the incident.

An Indian man once told miner Fred Beck that if he ever saw Selahtik to show that he was friendly. The way to express this was to wave cedar boughs at the Selahtik, so that it would then know that he had come in peace. Later Beck might have wished he had listened to his Indian friend's advice when he and a group of miners had their own encounter with the mythical beast.

Beck, his father-in-law, Marion Smith, brother-in-law, Roy Smith, Gabe LeFever, and John Peterson, were prospecting around Mount St. Helens in southwestern Washington, where they had sought gold for several years, when they had experiences both spiritual and terrifying. In 1922 they were on a gold-hunting expedition when a spiritual being in the form of an Indian man appeared to the members of the party. The Indian spirit told them that a white arrow would go before them to show them the way. When the miners referred to him as Great Spirit, the Indian replied, "The Great Spirit is above me. We are all of the Great Spirit, if we listen when the Great Spirit talks." The men followed the white arrow for four days, beginning at the Lewis River, south of Mount St. Helens, and traveling up the Muddy River. The terrain was rocky, rough, and rugged, making for very slow going up many steep slopes. One of the miners became tired and impatient and cursed the spirit that led them. Just then, they saw the white arrow soar upward, change direction, and descend downward. The arrow seemed to hover at the top of the north cliff of what later became known as Ape Canyon as a result of the men's adventures. As the group approached the site, they saw the image of an open door. Their spirit guide appeared before the opening and told them, "Because you have cursed the spirit leading you, you will be shown where there is gold, but it is not given to you." With that the apparition disappeared and the door began to close.

The men named their mine the Vander White, after another spirit they had encountered, the spirit of a woman who had comforted them on their journey. They proceeded to blast a mineshaft at the opening the white arrow had indicated, and to work the mine for two more years. An assay they had done showed that the mine contained $2,000 of gold per ton of rock, but Beck and his friends never found the main "pocket of gold" within the cliff.

Beck wrote of the group, "We were simple men and hard working men, and an aura of good or spiritual power surrounded us."

At first all was calm and peaceful, though sometimes the men would hear whistling, or hollow thudding-thumping noises coming from the woods. The sound usually came at night, but sometimes soft thumping sounds were heard during daylight hours. One of the prospectors became convinced that Beck was making the noise. This man led the way on most excursions, and when the noises were heard he quickly turned to Beck at the back of the group. This happened about eight times before he told the others, "By golly boys, it's not Fred making that noise after all." Still, he wanted to make sure that Beck was not playing a joke on him. After giving a false excuse, the miner walked away from camp to explore the source of the mysterious thudlike noises. When he returned to camp he announced to the others, "Now I'm certain it's none of us. I walked for half an hour and everywhere I went, I heard it. Sounds like there's a hollow drum in the earth somewhere and something is hitting it."

The men also saw unexplained giant humanlike tracks while camped in a tent below Pumy Butte. Camp was near a creek that flowed into a large, wet sandbar. They would go to the creek area to wash their dishes and get drinking water. After one such outing, one of the miners returned to camp in an agitated state. He led the others back to the sandbar and took them to its center. In the middle of the acrewide sandbar were two enormous tracks approximately four inches in depth. There wasn't another track on the entire sandbar. It looked as if whatever had made the impressions must have been dropped from the sky and taken back up.

At the time the miners dismissed the tracks as big Indians fishing barefoot along the river.

Marion Smith told of rumors he had heard about a man fishing the Muddy River. The fisherman laid out a string of the fish he had caught on the riverbank and went back to fishing the river. A sound made him turn to the riverbank where he saw a great man-like creature smashing the fish he had caught against the rocks. The fisherman rushed out of the woods, convinced that what he had seen was not human.

During their six years of prospecting in the Mount St. Helens and Lewis River area, the five miners spotted giant footprint-like tracks near creek beds and springs on other occasions. Smith, who was an experienced hunter and woodsman, was always nervous when the tracks were found. The prints were large (up to 19 inches long) and Smith knew of no animal that could have made them. But the track makers had left them alone and they felt safe enough. That changed when one among them accused their spirit guide of being a liar. From then on Beck admitted, "A quiet apprehensiveness settled over us." They continued to work the Vander White claim, but deep down each man felt that no good would come of it. The men built a log cabin and filled the cracks between the logs with chinking made from strips of split saplings. The cabin was built solidly enough to withstand the deep snows that winters dumped upon the peaks of the Cascade Range.

There was great excitement mid-July of 1924, after the Vander White partners had received the good assay on their claim. Though Beck had a toothache and asked Marion Smith, whose old Ford was their only mode of transportation, to take him to town to see a dentist, Smith refused. "God or the Devil" could not get him away from his claim he replied.

Smith was determined to continue mining even though the men had been hearing strange noises every evening for a week. Each night they heard a "shrill, peculiar whistling." First they would hear it echoing from one ridge top, followed by an answering whistle from a neighboring ridge. They also experienced the deep thumping noises, as if something was pounding itself on its chest.

Fearing whatever was out there, Smith asked Beck to come with him to get water from the creek, located about a hundred yards from their cabin. The apprehensive Smith suggested they take along their rifles for protection. As they walked toward the spring, Smith yelled and raised up his rifle. Beck saw what he was aiming at—a hairy creature about a hundred yards in front of them. A 7-foot-tall being, covered in dark black or brown hair, was standing next to a pine tree across a small canyon. The creature darted behind the tree, but as it poked its head out for a peek, Smith shot at it. Pieces of bark flew off of the tree with each of the three shots fired. The animal took off running down the ridge, upright, on two legs, at great speed. Beck took three more shots at it and gave chase before it disappeared from view. "Don't worry about that devil, Fred, I got him right in the head!" exclaimed Smith. As the men reached the ridge top, they were able to look down and see the creature running and leaping across distances of up to 14 feet. Neither man understood how the animal escaped unscathed with at least three bullets in its head.

The two took their water back to the log cabin and told their partners of the experience with the great apelike beast. All agreed it would be best to leave for home the next morning since it would be dark before they could get to the place they had left the car. They decided to spend one more night in the cabin, rather than be caught unprotected in the woods after sunset. The sturdy log cabin was windowless and contained a long bunk bed and a rock fireplace at one end. Two prospectors slept in the bunk, and three on pine boughs on the cabin floor.

All were asleep when around midnight they were awakened by a "tremendous thud against the cabin wall." Marion Smith, who had been sleeping on the cabin's floor, was yelling and kicking. Filling or chinking had been knocked loose from between the logs of the cabin and had fallen on his chest. Smith was waving the rifle that he slept next to back and forth as he thrashed about. Beck rushed over to his father-in-law and pulled the pieces of chinking off his chest. As Smith jumped to his feet, the men heard a tremendous amount of commotion from outside their shelter. They had a pile of unused pine shakes near the cabin, and it sounded like many feet were stomping and trampling over the pile of split wood. All of the miners had grabbed their rifles by that time. Smith peeked through the hole in the wall where the chinking had broken out. Though he saw only three of the giant, hairy creatures outside the cabin, it sounded "like a herd of horses," as if there were many more.

Throughout the night, the creatures hurled rocks at the log cabin. Most hit with an enormous bang, but then clattered harmlessly to the ground. A few did fall down the chimney into the fireplace. The men shot their rifles through the gap in the log cabin wall, but only when the beings were attacking their cabin. As the raiders backed off, the miners would stop shooting at them. Beck thought that if they saw that the men only shot at them when they charged at the cabin, they might realize that the men were just defending themselves and would not harm them if they left. That strategy changed when the men heard heavy footsteps above them, and realized that the creatures were on the cabin's roof. Round after round was fired through the ceiling. A long pole was stripped from the bunk bed and used to brace the log door. Still the attackers were butting up against the door, causing it to visibly vibrate from the impacts. Shots were fired through the thick, log-hewn door. The creatures shoved against the walls of the little cabin as if trying to push the structure over. Smith and Beck did almost all of the shooting; the three others huddled in a corner of the cabin with guns clutched in their fists, too shocked to fire.

The seemingly endless barrage of rock throwing and battering went on all night long. The most frightening moment came when a long, hairy arm came reaching through the space between the cabin's logs and grabbed one of the men's axes by its handle. Beck turned the head of the axe upright, so it stuck between the logs preventing the creature from pulling the axe out. Simultaneously Smith fired his rifle at the creature's arm, barely missing Beck's hand. The ax was dropped and Beck pulled it safely back inside the cabin where it could not be reached again.

During a lull in the fighting, Smith sang out, "If you leave us alone, we'll leave you alone, and we'll all go home in the morning." He truly thought that the Mountain Devils (his name for the beings) might understand and leave them in peace. Just before daylight the attack ended, and as soon as the partners were sure their enemies were gone and it was light enough to see, they ventured cautiously from their shelter. The ground around the cabin was completely covered with impressions of gigantic feet.

On their way to the mine tunnel to retrieve their tools, Beck spotted one of the "apelike creatures" approximately 80 yards from them at the edge of the canyon. Taking aim, with the creature plainly in his sights, he shot it three times in the back. Although Beck heard all three bullets hit and saw fur flying from its back, the ape started to run, then fell off of a cliff into a 400-foot gorge. After that Smith opined that they should leave immediately, without even packing up their mining equipment or supplies. He reasoned that it was better to leave $200 in supplies, powder, and drilling equipment behind than to lose their lives. All agreed and they packed out only what they could fit into their packsacks.

Beck thought that he had convinced the others not to speak of their experience, but as soon as they reached the Spirit Lake Ranger Station, his father-in-law let loose the tale. Smith walked to the ranger's quarters searching for Ranger Welch. When he had previously told Welch about the giant tracks he had seen in the mountain canyon, the ranger had asked him to report back to him if he ever encountered more. Smith first spoke to Mrs. Welch as the ranger was outside in the barn. The two men met outside the barn where Smith told Welch that he had shot a Mountain Devil. Welch asked the miner if he meant he had shot a bear. "No, a Mountain Devil," exclaimed the prospector. Welch asked if he was talking about a wolverine, to which Smith again answered, "No, a Mountain Devil!" At that the ranger became alarmed and surmised that the crazed miner might have shot his wife. The ranger was just contemplating how to wrest the rifle from Smith hands, when Mrs. Welch appeared on the porch. He then saw the other men still sitting in the car, tightly gripping their guns. Welch later described them as a bunch of wild-eyed miners. When the group headed for their homes in Kelso, they left a thoroughly puzzled ranger at the station with no idea what to make of their story.

The tale quickly spread around the town of Kelso after the miners' return. It wasn't long before the press got wind of the incident and it appeared in papers throughout Washington and Oregon. After that, as Beck described, "The Great Hairy Ape Hunt of 1924 was on." Many interviews followed, curious people came to Mount St. Helens seeking the Great Hairy Apes, or Mountain Devils. Beck even spoke to a big game hunter from England who showed him a gun so large that he guessed it must have been an elephant gun.

The day after the stories broke, the ranger from the Spirit Lake station announced his belief that boys from a local YMCA camp were responsible for the assault on the cabin. The ranger later retracted his statements when the boys had all been accounted for the night of the incident. After seeing the aftermath at the cabin, he changed his opinion as he did not think that mere boys could have inflicted the damage done there. Though he continued to believe that humans were responsible for the incident, the ranger did make the following statement to a reporter for the *Portland Oregonian*:

"Old man Smith, who started this ape stampede, absolutely believes it. If ever a man was 'wild-eyed,' it was Smith when he came down here from the cabin with a story of having been attacked by apes. Something happened up there, but I can't imagine what though. It wasn't apes. Another funny thing is that you can't shake the stories of the other men with Smith. Oh there's a mystery about it. The mystery to me is who put up the job on Smith and his companions and how in the world they did it."

Later Fred Beck went back to the cabin site with two reporters and detective from Portland. The group found the cabin in squalor, with rocks ringing the property, and a few scattered around the base of the fireplace. Though they did see large tracks, which they photographed and measured at 19 inches, they failed to find any of the "apemen." Nor did they find the bodies of the creatures that had been shot. Some believed the animals' remains were washed away by seasonal snow melt, or that their fellow beings came and removed the bodies, taking them back to their lava caves.

Over the years many accounts of the event were written, but Fred Beck disputed some of the stories. Some told of gigantic boulders being hurled at the log cabin during the great attack. Beck stated that though there were a few sizeable rocks found around the cabin, none amounted to the size of boulders. Most of the rocks thrown made quite a ruckus, but bounced off the sturdy pine logs siding the structure. It is not true that any huge rocks fell through the roof, but some did fall down the chimney and roll out of the fireplace. Neither Beck nor any of the miners were rendered unconscious by any of the falling rocks, as was sometimes reported. The log cabin stood for many years and was visited by many curious adventurers. It lasted until the 1960s when it was reduced to ashes by a fire.

In a 1966 interview with Roger Patterson (producer of the famous and controversial Sasquatch film), Beck described the apes as being about 8 feet tall and built like a man with a narrow waist, broad chests and shoulders, and "bull necks." Their noses were flat and ears similar to human ears. The bodies were covered with hair, with less on the faces and none on the palms of their hands. The apes' elongated arms hung down as far as their knees. They walked upright on two legs, their great weight causing deep impressions in the ground.

Stories about the event continued to be printed in local newspapers for over forty years. The *Longview Daily News* recounted the event on June 27 and 28, 1964, saying, "The legend of the apemen of Mt. St. Helens returns, like hay fever, with summer weather." Sightings in and around Ape Canyon abounded between 1963 and 1964, with two groups of Portland sightseers describing an encounter with a 7- to 10-foot-tall, light-colored hairy creature; three witnesses riding in a car spotted such a being in their headlights on a desolate mountain road; and a couple fishing on the Lewis River encountered a beige-colored figure "bigger than any human," which disappeared into the brush leaving a huge footprint in the sand.

Some believe that an elaborate prank was pulled off against the frightened miners in the summer of 1924. One man came forward saying he had made the tracks they saw with his knuckles. After the great influx of curious "ape hunters" around Ape Canyon, it became impossible to know what had been there before all of the publicity.

Others thought the whole story was a hoax made up by the miners to keep people away from their gold claim. Since the prospectors walked away from their mine, leaving hundreds of dollars in equipment behind, this seems unlikely. Beck claimed that none of the miners took any gold ore out of the Vander White mine, and that the few nuggets he left Ape Canyon with were picked up in other places.

The canyon's name was bestowed upon it as a result of the miners' experiences. Ape Canyon is a deep, desolate, rugged valley in a remote area, part of which was deluged by mudflows when the 1980 eruption of Mount St. Helens caused lahars or mudflows to cascade down the mountain clogging the Muddy River. One point of the canyon ends near Ape Cave,[1] the third longest lava tube in North America. Ape Cave contains 13,042 feet of mysterious chambers, lava falls, and oddly contoured walls. Marion Smith later said that he believed the cabin, which was built just a year before the Mountain Devil attack, had been constructed near a cave where the apes lived. Smith told an interviewer that he knew where the apes' caves were.

Was this remote area home to a lost tribe of giants and could they still live in Ape Canyon? Nearly all Washington tribes describe the same type of creatures, who have been heard making whistling noises like those the miners heard. Reverend Walker's 1840 letter contains references to a mammoth race of beings who were known to throw stones at Indian lodges in the night. Whether they're called Mountain Devils, Giant Apes, Big Foot, or Sasquatch, Beck predicted in his account of the Ape Canyon incident, "No one will ever capture one, and no one will ever kill one . . . so will they always get away."

---

1 Ape Cave was named by a troop of Boy Scouts, who were the first to explore the cave in the early 1950s, in honor of a group of foresters called the St. Helens Apes.

LADY OF THE LAKE

Deep, dark, beautiful and mysterious—Lake Crescent lies in a glacier-carved valley on the northern edge of the Olympic Peninsula. Minor peaks of the Olympic Mountains surround the lake, with the highest, Mount Storm King, overlooking it. According to legend the beauty of the region was marred by war when the Klallam and Quileute tribes fought a bloody battle in the glacial valley near the salt-water shores of the Strait of Juan de Fuca. For two days Mount Storm King witnessed the fighting and killing, becoming angrier and angrier at the bloodshed. The next day, Mount Storm King broke off a chunk of rock from his peak and threw it into the valley where the tribes were at war. All of the warriors were killed instantly. The giant boulder also dammed up the river that had flowed into the valley causing a clear, peaceful, crescent-shaped lake to form where there had been only bloodshed and war. Mount Storm King is mirrored in the clear blue waters of the lake he created and still guards.

Generations of Klallam and Quileute Indians would not go near Lake Crescent because they grew up hearing stories about the deaths of the many warriors who perished when the lake was created. Even today Klallam tribal members revere the lake for its history.

Tribal elders also teach their children to have the greatest respect for Lake Crescent, as many unexplainable things have happened there. One of those unexplainable mysteries was that Lake Crescent was bottomless and never gave up its dead. Those who drowned in the lake never returned to the surface and were forever lost. Or so it was told by generations of Klallam Indians and Olympic Peninsula natives until one summer day in 1940, when the lake did give up a corpse in a most unusual way.

Two brothers were fishing on Lake Crescent on July 6, 1940, when they noticed a large object floating off the shore near Sledgehammer Point. Powering their boat in for a closer look, the brothers were aghast at the sight they beheld. A 5-foot-long bundle, wrapped in blankets and bound with rope, floated on the lake's calm surface. A tear in the gray, striped blanket revealed an alabaster shoulder, and a foot protruded from the end of the wrap. The skin was so white that the body seemed more like a mannequin than human. The startled brothers immediately hit the boat's throttle and sped to shore to report their finding.

When Dr. Irving Kaveney, the Clallam County coroner, and Sheriff Charles Kemp examined the bundle, they made an even more amazing discovery. Before them lay the fully formed body of a woman in her mid-thirties. It was not bloated as drowning victims usually are. The total weight of the corpse was less than fifty pounds, and there was no odor of decomposition or decay. Dr. Kaveney claimed, "I never saw a corpse just like this one before. The flesh is hard, almost waxy. She must be nearly as large as when she went into the water. I'd say she is about 5 feet 6 inches in height and that she weighed about 140 pounds when alive." Sheriff Kemp gave the opinion: "It's more like a statue. The flesh has turned to some rubber-like substance."

But for the missing facial features, fingers and toes, the body was intact and had turned completely to soap.

Measured at 660 feet at their greatest depth, the frigid waters of Lake Crescent had preserved the woman's body. The sheer depth of the lake had prevented the growth of destructive bacteria or organisms that would normally feed on human flesh. Bodies long immersed in water lose their fat by leaching; this fat slowly combines with chemicals in the water to cause saponification, or the formation of soap. The floor of Lake Crescent was found to contain calcium and alkali, components of soap. Dr. Charles P. Larson, a pathologist called up from Tacoma to assist with the examination, provided the final explanation: "I will never forget looking at the Lady of the Lake for the first time. I'd never seen anything like it, but I'd read about things like it. Here was a body that had turned completely to soap. This is called adipocere formation, in which all the tissues of the body turn to soap. When they turn to soap, it's like that soap they advertise—it floats. . . . Adipocere formation is not the result of bacteria, but the result of chemical transformation of the tissues of the body over a long period of time. You make soap out of animal fat, calcium and alkali, and the water was alkaline at this depth, and there is calcium in all water. What had happened was a chemical change in the body—it may take several years for this to happen—in which all the tissues turned to soap."

The body was believed to have lain in an underwater stream that accelerated the saponification. According to Dr. Larson, "By soundings I found that underground stream which flows from Lake Crescent to Lake Sullivan. I got my sounding equipment down there and it stuck underneath a ledge where the current carried it into the stream. If you could ever get down underneath that ledge, you would probably find from fifty to one hundred bodies, all of which have turned to soap." When thrown into the lake, the corpse had been tied to weighted ropes that sank it to the floor of the seemingly bottomless mountain lake. Over time constant tension and deterioration of the ropes caused them to break; and the body, now composed entirely of buoyant soap, floated to the surface.

Who was this murder victim who had obviously been at the bottom of Lake Crescent for years? Remnants of a green wool dress with a JCPenney tag, stockings, and an elastic garter clung to the ivory corpse. A shock of auburn hair crowned the head, and a ring of bruises circled the neck. One thing was clear: The woman had been strangled before her body was dumped into the lake.

Local authorities were at a loss to identify the woman. The nameless woman's body lay in the county morgue for two months, after which she was buried in a pauper's grave at the Clallam County Cemetery. As more experts were summoned, the corpse was exhumed twice for further examination.

Noted Olympia criminologist Hollis B. Fultz, a special investigator from the Washington state attorney general's office, was called in to investigate the discovery of what the press dubbed "The Lady of the Lake." Fultz looked at reports of persons missing from the area and, on a hunch, zeroed in on a missing waitress from Port Angeles, a town 20 miles east of Lake Crescent.

Hallie Illingworth had been thirty-six at the time she disappeared. She was an attractive woman, 5 feet, 6 inches tall, with

Portrait of Hallie Illingworth taken shortly
before her death   BERT KELLOGG COLLECTION OF
THE NORTH OLYMPIC LIBRARY SYSTEM

auburn hair. Illingworth was reported missing when she failed
to show up for work one day. At the time of her disappearance,
her husband, Monty, told local people that she had run off with a
Navy lieutenant commander from Bremerton.

Fultz found this story unlikely, as Hallie had never trans-
ferred her union card. He tracked down a sister living near Walla

Walla. The sister told him that the last time she had seen Hallie was the week before Christmas 1937. Hallie had visited her one afternoon, departing in the early evening. Later that night, Monty had come to the sister's apartment looking for his wife. The next morning he again came looking for his spouse at the sister's place of employment. He was described as being extremely disheveled—looking like he had slept in his clothes. Monty explained that he had been drinking all night in Port Townsend. He said that he and Hallie had fought when he returned from his night of partying and that she had stormed out of their home. "Hallie's left me. After our big fight she packed a suitcase and said she was never coming back. She said none of us would ever see her again," he told Hallie's sister.

Though he told everyone that Hallie had left him, five months after her disappearance Monty filed for divorce on grounds of incompatibility rather than desertion. On August 3, 1938, he was granted an interlocutory divorce by default, since Hallie could not be found to respond to the petition.

Investigator Fultz discovered a friend and former coworker of Hallie's who ran a cookhouse for a timber mill in Lake Pleasant. The friend described Hallie as frequently showing up to work her waitressing shift with black-and-blue marks on her face and neck. Hallie told her coworkers that her husband had choked her and broken a tooth out of her upper dental plate. When shown photos of the body, the friend recognized not only the auburn hair and shape of the figure, but the green wool JCPenney dress. She went on to describe bunions on Hallie's right foot that matched those on the corpse.

Fultz located another of Hallie's sisters in Vancouver, Washington. When shown photos of the Lady of the Lake, this sister believed that the hair color and visible features were a match for those of Hallie. "That's Hallie's form, all right. And she had high cheekbones like the photos show. Her hair was exactly the color of this," the sister told Fultz. She also mentioned that Hallie had worn a partial upper plate. A six-tooth upper plate had been found in the mouth of the body.

Though it was fairly certain that the Lady of the Lake was Hallie Illingworth, Fultz investigated further. A chart was made of the upper plate and advertisements were placed in national dental journals asking the dentist who had made the appliance to come forward. These ads, picturing the bridgework, ran for months with no success. More than a year later, a South Dakota dentist answered the ad, claiming that he had made a partial upper denture thirteen years earlier for a Hallie Spraker. Mrs. Spraker had left her first husband and moved to the Pacific Northwest without reimbursing the dentist for his work. The South Dakota dentist also told them that the woman he treated had no molars at all in her lower jaw. Neither did the corpse.

The citizens of Port Angeles remembered a woman named Hallie who had been briefly married to Donald Strickland, her second husband, with whom she had operated a Seattle restaurant for about a year before moving to Port Angeles. Hallie had been a waitress at the Lake Crescent Tavern, now part of Lake Crescent Lodge in the Olympic National Park. She met Monty J. Illingworth, a Port Angeles beer distributor, in the Lake Crescent Tavern.

Lake Crescent Tavern, Lake Crescent, Washington, ca. 1918 UNIVERSITY OF WASHINGTON LIBRARIES, SPECIAL COLLECTIONS, UW 12027

On June 16, 1936, the waitress and the beer truck driver were married. Townspeople remembered the couple's binge drinking episodes and violent battles fueled by the jealous rages of both parties. Many recalled witnessing black eyes and bruises on Hallie's neck. When Hallie disappeared in late 1937, Monty explained her absence by saying she had run off to Alaska with a sailor. Shortly after his wife's disappearance, he moved to Long Beach, California, with the daughter of a wealthy Port Angeles timber magnate. Coincidentally, timber heiress Elinore Pearson had been the roommate of one of Hallie's sisters. For years Pearson continued to correspond with the sister, always asking if she had heard from Hallie.

Authorities were convinced that the Lady of the Lake was Hallie Illingworth. Now, they had to prove who had killed her.

Hollis Fultz identified the rope that had bound Hallie's body as being of a type that had been sold exclusively by Sears Roebuck in Port Angeles. Sifting through the sales records at Sears, Fultz found that a Lake Crescent resort owner had purchased 1,000 feet of the rope for tying up his rental boats. Investigators went to the La Poel Resort on the west shore of Lake Crescent to interview the resort owner, Harry Brooks. Dr. Larson questioned Brooks until he was satisfied that the resort owner was not involved in the murder. He was about to leave the resort when suddenly Brooks remembered a key detail. Brooks told them that he had loaned one hundred feet of the rope to a beer salesman, who said that he needed it to pull his truck out of the mud. The beer truck driver neither returned the rope nor paid for it. Brooks provided the investigators with a length of the same rope that he had loaned out to the driver of the stuck truck. Dr. Larson performed forensic tests on Brooks's rope and made comparisons to the rope found binding the body. Tests proved that the fiber they were made from was the same pure hemp: The two ropes had the exact same strand count and twist and were the same size. It was now certain that the ropes wrapped around Hallie's body came from the very same rope that beer truck driver Monty Illingworth had borrowed from the La Poel Resort.

Monty J. Illingworth was found driving a bus in Long Beach. He and Elinore Pearson were living together and held themselves out to the community as husband and wife. Enough evidence had accumulated against Illingworth to convince the governor of California to sign an extradition order on November 3, 1941, and he was returned to Clallam County to stand trial for the murder of Hallie Latham Spraker Strickland Illingworth.

The sensational jury trial lasted nine days and drew national attention. The Clallam County attorney who prosecuted Illingworth had been his divorce lawyer and had filed his petition for dissolution against the absent Mrs. Illingworth. Dr. Larson's testimony and enthusiastic demonstrations about his forensic tests on the rope, the clothing, and the body were instrumental in the prosecution's case. At one point Dr. Larson requested a glass of water into which he dropped a piece of saponified tissue cut from the body. The sample sank directly to the bottom of the glass, but then began to rise until it floated at the top. This, he testified, was what Hallie's body had done when the deteriorated rope let go of it, allowing the soap corpse to float to the top of Lake Crescent.

After a short deliberation, Monty J. Illingworth was found guilty of murder in the second degree on March 5, 1942. Since the jury had determined that the murder was a crime of passion rather than one of premeditation, he had been convicted of the lesser charge. He was sentenced to life in prison at the Washington State Penitentiary in Walla Walla, but was paroled on January 10, 1951, after just nine years behind bars. Illingworth returned to California where he lived until his death more than twenty years later.

Though skilled investigators eventually solved the mystery, the mystique of the Lady of the Lake remains strong on the Olympic Peninsula at Lake Crescent. If Dr. Larson was correct, perhaps the clear, deep waters of the lake hold the saponified bodies of as many as one hundred victims who may never be found.

A WORLD-FAMOUS LOBOTOMY

Perhaps the most famous photograph of a frontal lobotomy was taken at Western State Hospital in Steilacoom. The photo shows a doctor hammering an ice-pick-like device called a leucotome into a woman's eye as a crowd of health-care workers watches. Dr. Walter Freeman was the inventor of the transorbital lobotomy, which he believed would cure mental illness. "Lobotomy gets them home," was his oft-repeated motto. The neurologist/psychiatrist would render his patient unconscious with several electric shocks from an electroshock therapy apparatus. Once the patient was unconscious, the doctor would lift the eyelid and insert the leucotome through a tear duct. The ice-pick-type instrument was then struck with a surgical hammer until it pierced the bone. Dr. Freeman then pushed the device into the frontal lobe of the brain and moved it back and forth before repeating the procedure through the other eye.

Dr. Freeman performed over 3,000 lobotomies during his career. He so believed that his transorbital lobotomy could cure any type of mental illness and return people to normal lives outside of mental institutions that he traveled the country demonstrating his procedure to doctors and nurses at psychiatric hospitals from coast to coast.

While no one disputes the fact that Dr. Freeman performed many lobotomies during his career, there remains much controversy regarding the individual patient in the famous photograph taken at Western State Hospital. Dr. Freeman claimed that his notorious lobotomy picture was of Seattle-born movie star Frances Farmer. Dr. Freeman's son swore that his father had told him the starlet was the patient in the photo.

The Farmer family and some Western State Hospital personnel deny that Frances Farmer ever had a frontal lobotomy. Did Frances Farmer suffer a lobotomy in addition to other egregious indignities at Washington's oldest mental asylum? The actress was "treated" with electroshock therapy and hydrotherapy, in which a sheet-wrapped patient is submerged in a tub of ice water for hours. The beautiful Farmer was allegedly physically and sexually abused by orderlies, who also sold her to drunken soldiers from Fort Lewis. How did a once promising Hollywood star come to endure such horrors?

Frances Elena Farmer was born in Seattle on September 19, 1913, the daughter of Lillian and Ernest M. Farmer, a Seattle lawyer. She grew up in a small house in West Seattle and graduated from West Seattle High School. Her parents had a volatile relationship, with Ernest moving in and out of the family home. As a senior in high school, Frances showed a talent for writing and won a $100 prize from Scholastic Magazine for her essay "God Dies." The press in the Northwest spread the news that a Seattle student had denied God and won a prize for it. This may have been the first time Farmer shocked society with her views, but it would not be the last.

Frances Farmer, ca. 1937   University of Washington
Libraries, Special Collections, UW 23919

At the University of Washington, she was a journalism major and student reporter for the *Daily* as a freshman in 1931. Since her father's law practice was not doing well, the young college student paid her way through a series of odd jobs. She worked in a perfume factory, waited tables, posed for art students, and served as an usherette at Seattle's ornate Paramount Theater and as a singing waitress at Paradise Lodge on Mount Rainier. Through another student reporter from the university's drama department, Farmer was introduced to a young drama instructor who convinced her to try acting. Though she had no experience acting, Farmer made a name for herself as a star in college plays. The stunning actress now had a burning desire to perform on Broadway in New York. To that end she entered a contest sponsored by the *Voice of Action*, a radical, Communist-leaning Seattle newspaper. Farmer won a trip to Moscow, Russia, via New York in March 1935. The local press labeled Farmer a Communist sympathizer with her own mother condemning her in print. The only real goal that Farmer had was to pursue an acting career in New York. In spite of opinions against her, she left school and Seattle on March 30, 1935.

The trip to Russia was the turning point in Farmer's career. Upon her return from Moscow to New York, she turned in her return bus ticket to Seattle in exchange for money, found a place to live, and set out looking for work as an actress. Through a friend from the Russia trip, she was introduced to agent Shepard Traube, who arranged a screen test, which led to a contract with Paramount Studios.

The budding star was featured in four movies in 1936 and married a handsome actor named William Anderson, who later became known on screen as Leif Erickson. Farmer arrived back in Seattle that year for the premiere of her movie, *Come and Get It*. Opening the movie in the star's hometown was a unique honor that Hollywood rarely bestowed on a new arrival. The City of Seattle welcomed her with an elegant reception at its finest hotel, The Olympic. She made appearances at the University of Washington and Paramount Theater and met the mayor, a senator, and the governor of the state. Of her return to the Paramount, Farmer noted caustically that a great emphasis was put on the fact that her name was lit up on the marquee of the theater where she had once worked as an usherette. Even as Seattle feted its native daughter, members of the press described their encounters with Farmer as being difficult and her behavior as temperamental and demanding. She refused to sign autographs at the Bon Marché and annoyed local newspaper reporters and government officials with her arrogance and sarcasm.

Still, Frances Farmer went on to star in Broadway plays and many movies, including *Toast of New York* with Cary Grant; *Rhythm on the Range* with Bing Crosby; *Son of Fury* with Tyrone Power; *World Premiere* with John Barrymore; and *The Bad Lands of Dakota* with Robert Stack. By the age of twenty-eight, she had made nineteen movies and acted in three Broadway plays and seven stock productions. Her marriage to William Anderson had begun to fall apart after just one year, and he would later divorce her on grounds of desertion.

As her fame grew, the rising star began to get a reputation for being a high-strung, temperamental actress who was prone to tantrums on the set. A pattern of heavy drinking and amphetamine indulgence accelerated after a failed love affair with a married playwright. Frances admitted that alcohol brought all of her suppressed anger to the surface and triggered erratic behavior.

By fall of 1942 Farmer had been arrested in Santa Monica and charged with drunken driving, driving without a license, and failing to observe a wartime dim-out zone by leaving her headlights on. She paid a portion of the fine and received a suspended sentence. While working on a movie set in January 1943, the volatile actress slapped her hairdresser causing a jaw injury. Farmer was also involved in a fight at a hotel bar. An outstanding warrant was then discovered for failure to pay all of her fine on the prior driving charges or report to her parole officer. According to Associated Press reports, when the detective and policewoman arrived at her hotel to arrest her, she asked if she might first take a bath. The request was granted, but Farmer managed to embarrass the arresting officer by emerging naked from the bathroom.

The Seattle Times reported, "It was no movie glamour girl who faced the bench . . . her light blue suit was mussed, her blond hair straggling, her eyes were red."

The judge asked the starlet if she had been drinking since her last appearance in his court, to which she shouted her answer out, "Yes, I drank everything I could get, including Benzedrine." Then the judge began his admonishment, telling the defendant that she had been advised against drinking even one drink of liquor or failing to be a law-abiding citizen. Her outburst cut him off as Farmer screamed, "What do you expect me to do? I get liquor in my orange juice, in my coffee. Must I starve to death to obey your laws?"

At that the judge sentenced her to 180 days in jail, but when she was denied permission to use a telephone a total melee began. She threw an inkwell at the bench and commenced to tear apart the room. She was carried from the courtroom kicking and screaming. Ultimately it took five officers and a straitjacket to contain her fury. A picture of her fighting with officers as they removed her from the court became a front-page newspaper item across the country.

After she'd spent one night in jail, the Farmer family and a psychiatrist had her admitted to a hospital mental ward in Los Angeles. From there she was committed to the Screen Actors' Sanitarium where she endured insulin shock therapy for her diagnosed condition of manic-depressive psychosis. In her autobiography Farmer described receiving ninety insulin shock treatments for ninety days. She stated that the effect was a brutal physical attack that stunned brain cells and left her body nauseated and in pain. Farmer's mother had her daughter released to her custody in Seattle after about six months of hospitalization.

Farmer and her mother had never gotten along well. During her stay at the Farmer home in West Seattle, the two fought constantly and Farmer continued to drink until her mother had her committed to Harborview Hospital for evaluation. Lillian Farmer filed an "insanity complaint" in King County Superior Court asking to have her daughter committed. *The Seattle Times* reported that her mother testified Farmer would have "hysterical attacks and send for doctors." Two doctors gave testimony to the effect that when Farmer started drinking she became "agitated and delusional." The diagnosis was a form of schizophrenia.

Judged insane, on March 24, 1944, Frances Farmer was committed by court order to Western State Hospital at Steilacoom. Her "insanity" was treated with electroconvulsive shock therapy, which she endured several times a week. Rendered disoriented, with a deadened mind and limited recall, she was pronounced completely cured and sent home in July to the custody of her mother.

Farmer described living with her mother under strained circumstances as being an isolated existence that caused her further mental deterioration. After a physical battle with her mother and father and a drunken episode, Lillian called an ambulance and had Frances transported to the hospital at Steilacoom once again. She was committed the morning of May 22, 1945. Her confinement would last five years this time.

Western State Hospital, formerly Washington State Hospital for the Insane, was built on the grounds of old Fort Steilacoom. The buildings were ancient, out of date, and insufficient to house the number of patients they did. Fewer than twenty doctors and twenty fully trained nurses cared for nearly 3,000 infirm. As an inmate in a state asylum for the insane, Farmer claimed she experienced intolerable terror. She reported she was poisoned with tainted food, gnawed on by rats, molested by orderlies, plunged into ice water baths, strapped into straitjackets, and chained in padded cells. Because she was a repeat admission to the mental hospital, she said, she was sent directly to the back wards where the hopelessly insane were kept. She was housed in antiquated, crumbling barracks with rough-hewn floors, boarded-up windows, and leaky roofs. Winters on the wards were cold and damp or icy, and summers stifling, as heat filled the decaying buildings with insects and exacerbated the unbearable stench of the rooms.

Patients were subjected to abuse from other inmates, trustees, and orderlies. Farmer wrote that every inmate had experienced violent attacks at the asylum. Though she doesn't elaborate, she describes strange men being smuggled into the women's wards for such assaults. The 1983 movie *Frances*, starring Jessica Lange, depicts Farmer being held down by orderlies and assaulted by soldiers.

On her ward Farmer claimed that naked women were chained, confined by straitjackets and tied in sacks or had their heads hooded to restrain them. Frequent riots were quelled by shooting torrents of water through thick hoses at the inmates. Patients were also punished by confinement to a solitary existence in tiny, dark, unheated, closetlike rooms.

Western State Hospital in the 1940s was certainly a run-down, overcrowded facility where the patients were undersupervised at an understaffed hospital that amounted to a warehouse for the mentally ill. Doctors were desperate for methods to treat their institutionalized patients and send them home. Into this environment came the publicity-seeking Dr. Walter Freeman to demonstrate his transorbital lobotomy technique. After his classes, Dr. Freeman's ice-pick lobotomies were often taken up and performed by psychiatrists with little or no surgical experience.

One day in 1949 Dr. Freeman gave a lecture on his transorbital lobotomies to an audience of Western State Hospital staff, psychiatrists, and other curious viewers. Thirteen women on gurneys were lined up before the students. As each woman was wheeled before Dr. Freeman, he attached electrodes to her head and administered shock treatment until the patient passed out. He then hammered his leucotome through the patient's eye socket, rotated the instrument, and then pulled it from the woman's eye. These assembly-line lobotomies continued until Dr. Freeman had operated on all thirteen women as his audience looked on with amazement and revulsion. One of the onlookers took a picture of Dr. Freeman hammering his instrument into a woman's eye socket. Dr. Freeman reportedly often showed this

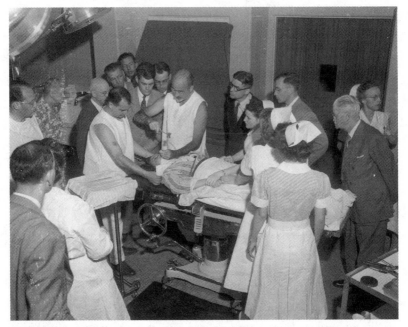

Dr. Walter Freeman performing a lobotomy at Western State Hospital, Steilacoom, July 6, 1949 *SEATTLE POST-INTELLIGENCER* COLLECTION, MUSEUM OF HISTORY & INDUSTRY

photo to friends, claiming the subject was Frances Farmer. The photograph circulated widely and became the most famous picture of a lobotomy ever published.

Farmer was released at her parents' request in late March 1950. Her aging parents summoned their long-suffering daughter to care for them in their West Seattle home after Lillian had endured a stroke. Farmer obliged, though she harbored great resentment toward the two who had incarcerated her for five years. Her parents kept their nursemaid hostage with constant threats of sending her back to the asylum if she did not comply with their demands. Farmer later learned that her father had had the court declare her legally competent in 1951, but he had failed to inform her of this fact, keeping her at her parent's mercy.

The woman who had been feted at the Olympic Hotel as Seattle's own Hollywood star was forced to take employment at the five-star hotel as a laundry maid for 75 cents an hour to support her mother. After a brief, failed marriage in Seattle in 1954, she sent her mother off to a sister and moved to California where she worked as a secretary and hotel clerk. Farmer entered into a short third marriage with a man she met in 1957, who convinced her to attempt to revive her acting career. She then appeared in several television, movie, and stage productions and on the *Ed Sullivan Show*. In 1958 Farmer moved to Indianapolis where she hosted an afternoon TV show and taught acting at Purdue University. Her attempt at a stable life was lost when she began drinking heavily and acting erratically, culminating in a drunken-driving crash and arrest in 1964.

Frances Elena Farmer was diagnosed with cancer of the esophagus and died on August 1, 1970, before she could finish writing her autobiography.

Undoubtedly, the former screen star suffered terribly while incarcerated in the Washington state "insane asylum." Did all of the horrors she and others described really occur? *The Seattle Times* published the accounts of three psychiatric nurses who had worked at Western State Hospital. These women disputed many of the depictions of the hospital as portrayed in the movie *Frances* and in books by and about Farmer.

As to the portrayal of naked women chained in cagelike rooms, Mary Burchett, a nurse at Western State Hospital from

1939 to 1972, said, "I never saw people naked there." Actress Jessica Lange is shown in the film being assaulted by World War II–era soldiers, but another nurse, Ethel Sass, stated that she did not see a soldier at the hospital at any time. Beverly Tibbetts, hospital nurse from 1947 to 1982, was quoted, "I never heard of anybody bringing in a truckload of soldiers until the book came out." The book she referred to was a biography entitled *Shadowland* by *Post-Intelligencer* film critic William Arnold. Tibbetts also swore that men and women were kept strictly segregated at the Steilacoom facilities.

While the three nurses were sure Farmer had been treated with electroshock treatments, they disputed the book and movie depictions of a lobotomy being performed on her. The movie showed Farmer as one of the women being operated on in front of an audience at the asylum. Her biographer, Arnold, claimed that Dr. Freeman performed Farmer's lobotomy separately to preserve her privacy. Before he died, Dr. Freeman told his son that Frances Farmer was the patient obtaining a lobotomy in his famous photo. Farmer's sister, Edith, who also penned a biography, denied that Frances ever had such an operation. Edith wrote that when her father visited the hospital in August 1947, the doctors proposed performing a lobotomy on his daughter. He wrote to Edith that he had gotten there "just in time to head them off from some danged experimental brain operation on her. I notified them one and all if they tried any of their guinea pig operations on her they would have a danged big law suit on their hands." According to her father the "head man" agreed that nothing would happen to Farmer without his written consent.

Some claim that Farmer's dull, flat demeanor and memory lapses were the result of a Freeman lobotomy. By her own admission, her memory loss could be attributed to the insulin and electroshock treatments. Her lack of emotionalism could easily have been due to the horrors of years of confinement in the mental institution. Nurse Tibbetts was quoted by the *Times*, "I'm sure Frances Farmer didn't have one. I worked on all the patients who had lobotomies, and Frances Farmer never came to that ward."

In his book, biographer Arnold described Dr. Freeman asking witnesses to leave the room before he hammered his ice-pick-type instrument into Farmer's brain. Arnold then concluded, "no one will ever know exactly what happened next."

CAPTAIN INGALLS'S GOLD

Lost in the eastern Cascade Mountains in the winter of 1872, Captain Benjamin Ingalls of the United States Army Cavalry meandered slowly up a steep, narrow trail hoping that the view from the cliff top might afford him his bearings. The captain had been wandering the vast Cascade wilderness for days, having become separated from the other soldiers in his unit.

From the ridge top, Ingalls was able to see down the canyon walls to a series of three alpine lakes below, all connected by a mountain creek. While the outer two lakes appeared dark and bottomless, the middle lake was a lighter, sparkling, emerald color. Drawn to the unusual crescent-shaped body of water, the captain descended into the canyon. He found the shores of the glittering lake lined with shimmering gold ore imbedded in quartz stone. The captain judged that ten tons of gold lay on the surface of the ground, and even more must be buried below.

Now unconcerned about reuniting with his unit, Ingalls camped on the lake's bank for several days. While there, he took samples of the golden ore and surveyed and mapped the canyon and lakebed. Ingalls buried his map at the mouth of what is now known as Ingalls Creek near Mount Stuart. He then followed the creek out of the canyon.

Still lost in the dense wilderness, Captain Ingalls made camp a few miles away from the mouth of the creek. A full, winter moon shown eerily over a calm, clear night. Around 10 p.m. on December 14, 1872, he was awakened by an intense rumbling noise emanating from deep within the earth. Then, the thundering sound of an enormous explosion echoed throughout the mountains. His terrified horse reared up, straining at his tether and squealing with fear as the ground rumbled and shook while enormous boulders smashed down the mountainsides.

This powerful earthquake rocked central Washington for nearly three minutes and was followed by many aftershocks. Shaking was felt from Oregon to Canada, and Walla Walla to Seattle. The shallow quake shook the surface of the earth with an intensity not felt since then. To this date, the 6.8 temblor stands as Washington's largest crustal earthquake.

Local Wenatchee Indians attributed the phenomena to "mad bulls down in the earth." The earthquake of 1872 changed central Washington's landscape in a sudden and violent manner. Half a mountain near the town of Entiat broke loose and dropped into the Columbia River damming the river south of it and creating Ribbon Cliff. At the confluence of the Columbia and Chelan Rivers, a geyser erupted from the earth shooting water 20 feet into the air. In a Chelan Indian encampment, the ground ruptured causing sulfuric gas to escape into the air and spoil the tribe's winter food stores. A mountain east of the Columbia split open and began to spew black oil.

Ingalls and his horse endured the intense shaking, listening to the roar of mountainsides breaking loose, boulders crashing

Ingalls Lake reflects Mount Stuart   Alan Bauer Photography

downward, branches splitting off and uprooted trees falling for what seemed an eternity. Since he did not know the extent of the damage caused by the great earthquake of 1872, it likely did not occur to Ingalls that his canyon lakes might have been buried under the tons of rock rained down from the sides of the Cascades.

Captain Ingalls never got the chance to return to his mountain lake lined with gold. He was shot to death shortly after rejoining his cavalry unit. Before his death Ingalls wrote to a friend telling him of his discovery and the location of the buried map and sent enticing samples of gold ore to prove his claim. He asked his friend, John Hansel, to join him on a second expedition to the alpine lakes. Although Hansel searched the area for years, he was never able to find the buried map or the lake lined with gold.

Or so goes the myth of Captain Ingalls's gold. This vivid account of Captain Ingalls's gold find, which has intrigued treasure hunters for more than 100 years, has somehow become inextricably intertwined with tales of the great earthquake of 1872. Since Ingalls died in 1861, we know that he had to have discovered the gold at an earlier date. Seismic activity was known to have occurred in central Washington in the 1850s. He must have experienced an earlier seismic event, but a landslide resulting from the quake of 1872 could have permanently covered the lost treasure. Perhaps this explains how Ingalls's discovery became part of the lore of the great quake.

Captain Ingalls was known to have mounted at least two expeditions to central Washington, the first in 1855, and the second in 1861. Although no written record exists of the original discovery, we do know that Ingalls and his soldiers were in the Wenatchee Mountains in 1855, and a first-hand account of Ben Ingalls's return trip to the area to retrieve his fortune has been preserved in a narrative given by his friend John Hansel. Exactly when and where Ingalls found his lakes of gold are the subject of many myths and tales. The facts known about Ingalls's travels through the Wenatchee Mountains are as follows.

When Washington became a territory in 1853, the first territorial governor, Isaac I. Stevens, ordered surveys of the Cascades and beyond, seeking passes for portage over the mountains. Captain Benjamin Ingalls headed a unit of more than 200 men—surveyors, and soldiers to guard their safety—through the Wenatchee Mountains in 1855. It could have been on this detail that Ingalls became separated from his men and discovered the rich placer ore and gold quartz lakebed. Ingalls is said to be the first person to have discovered gold in the region, though no gold find was reported by anyone on the survey expedition. Gold had been discovered near Colville and on the Fraser River in British Columbia between 1855 and 1858, and many hopeful prospectors seeking riches were caught up in the gold rush northward.

It is known that during the spring of 1861, Ingalls left his home in Portland, Oregon, with a small group of men, including his son, Ben, and friends John Hansel and Jack Knot, on a prospecting expedition. They began by following trails along the southern banks of the Columbia River. The Ingalls group soon encountered fifty to sixty prospectors traveling with a hundred mules. For a fee Ingalls agreed to keep the mules shod and to travel with the group to a gold camp in Canada. Traveling with a larger group would ensure safety for the small band of friends. All the while Ingalls had a plan to detour from the miners at Peshastin. He would then find his lake lined with gold quartz, stake his claim, and rejoin the larger group.

After a difficult journey up the Columbia, the party camped on the eastern shore of the river near the mouth of the Wenatchee River to rest before pushing on into Canada. As the majority of the men rested, Ingalls grew agitated. Breaking away from camp, he took his son, Ben, John Hansel, Jack Knot, and a few more men across the Columbia River in canoes. All but Hansel thought they were merely exploring the scenic area. Hansel knew enough of the plan to know that Ingalls intended to follow the Wenatchee River to Peshastin Creek. Once there, Ingalls would travel on alone across the Wenatchee to find his lost ore, while the others continued up the river. Though he did not know exactly where his friend was going, Hansel knew that Ingalls had two days' worth of provisions with him for his solo journey.

Spring sunshine sparkled on the water and warmed the backs of the explorers making the expedition a thoroughly enjoyable outing. The young men of the party joked and laughed as they rowed up the river. Thinking they were just sightseeing, the men didn't understand Captain Ingalls's anxiety as he urged them to hurry onward. The group made their way along the shore between the water below and a sandstone cliff above them. Carrying a pick, shovel, and two days' provisions for his solitary exploration, Ingalls led the men quickly along.

Ducking low under the limbs of a low-hanging willow tree, Ingalls managed to avoid being hit in the face by the tree's branches; but, as he passed under the tree, his pick snagged on the willow. Ingalls called back a warning to Jack Knot, the man following his lead, "Look out, Jack!" In addition to his supplies, Jack was carrying an old muzzle-loading rifle with the barrel pointed forward as he walked. Knot heard the warning too late to heed it. The same willow branch that had snagged Ingalls's pick blew backward catching the hammer of the rifle held by Knot and discharging a round. A fifty-caliber bullet slammed into Captain Ingalls's back, penetrating near his spine and lodging in his stomach.

His men carried the mortally wounded captain back to the Columbia River camp on a makeshift stretcher. Ingalls lingered on for two days with his friend, John Hansel, at his side. On his death bed Ingalls confided the details of his secret plan to Hansel. He outlined the route to the area where his discovery lay, describing the trails, canyon, lakes, creek, and necessary landmarks.

Wenatchee Valley pioneer Jewell Sinclair related Ingalls's deathbed statements as told to her by Hansel:

"He described the landmarks and the directions and distance from creek to peak. He told John that when he had time he must hunt up 'them rich diggins'—rich gold quartz and placer—which were about one day's travel apart."

Ingalls asked his son to return his men to Portland and to tell his mother what had happened to her husband. The younger Ingalls was also instructed to travel with Hansel when he came back to central Washington to hunt for the gold.

Captain Ingalls died two days after the shooting accident. His men buried him across from the mouth of the Wenatchee River on the Columbia's eastern bank. Ben Jr. led the Ingalls party's return to Portland to break the news of his father's death to his mother.

Though Hansel was the only person to get a firsthand account of the gold find, he was never able to locate the area Ingalls described or find the beaches lined with gold quartz nuggets. The three lakes were thought by some to be parallel to the creek now bearing Captain Ben Ingalls's name. Others believed the find was higher up in the Wenatchee Range between Table Mountain and Tip-Top Peak. Ingalls Creek runs through the northeastern slopes of the Stuart Range, flowing toward Snow Lakes and the Enchantment Lake area, and south of Icicle Creek. The headwaters of the creek form at Ingalls Lake. Hansel and his family homesteaded near Ingalls Creek and mounted many expeditions in search of the lost treasure.

The lost lakes of gold may have been covered by the great quake of 1872, or by an earlier rockslide created by seismic activity. Whether lost or buried, the lakes of gold have never been found by John Hansel or anyone since.

SHANGHAIED!

Fifteen-year-old Harry Long left his Seattle house on Union Street December 21, 1901, and vanished. When Harry failed to return home by the next day, his parents filed a missing persons report with the Seattle Police Department. Worried, they told the authorities that Harry was not the type to run away, plus all of his clothes and possessions were still in his room. Harry was on his way to work when he disappeared, but he was known to stop and watch the ships in Elliott Bay along the way. The Long family believed that habit might have gotten young Harry shanghaied.

During the week of January 4, 1901, the names of eleven people, all but one men, were listed as missing in *The Seattle Star*. The newspaper routinely published the names and hometowns of missing persons given to them by the Seattle Police Department, which received a steady stream of inquiries from outside of Washington about missing loved ones. It was common for men to arrive on the West Coast, only to disappear. Did some, or all, of these men fall victim to the practice of shanghaiing?

"Shanghai," the verb, is defined as "to put aboard a ship by force." The term originated in San Francisco and referred to the end destination of many of the ships carrying crews obtained in just that manner. It was big business up and down the West Coast for crimps to make a good income by kidnapping or selling incapacitated men into servitude on outward-bound ships. In 1895, the United States government attempted to end the practice by passing a law that required sailors to read and sign the ship's articles before hiring onto a crew. Federal law defined "shanghai-ing" as the employment of any sailor who had not signed the ship's articles, or who had signed unwilling or drunkenly.

Lurid stories were told of sailors who were shanghaied from San Francisco, Portland, Tacoma, and Seattle, but by far the most notorious and prolific port of all was Port Townsend. Well-known, respected citizens of Port Townsend became very wealthy by running sailors boarding houses from which their agents or crimps supplied ships in the harbor with crews. Many of these boarding houses, brothels, and bars were built over piers with trap-doors that opened to the saltwater below. The human cargo could easily be dropped through the hatch into a waiting rowboat and transported quietly out to a deep-water ship in the bay. The good citizens of Port Townsend seemed unconcerned about lowlife, waterfront rats who were given drugged drinks and sent out to sea. After all it helped to clean up their lovely town with its elaborate, Victorian-style houses on the hill. John Sutton's story illustrates what could happen to an unsuspecting young man who wandered into Port Townsend.

When his logging camp shut down because of summer for-est fires, twenty-three-year-old logger John Sutton headed to the nearest town for recreation. Sutton went straight to Water Street in Port Townsend where good, bootleg Canadian whiskey, girls, and gambling were plentiful. At the Blue Light Saloon on Union Dock, he entered into a card game with a deserter from a British warship. When the naive logger had lost his last coin, the English gambler nodded at the bartender, who poured him a drink "on the house." As soon as the knockout drops in the special drink took effect, the crew went to work. After everything of value had been stripped and stolen from him (including his logging boots), Sutton was dropped through a trapdoor on the pier under the tavern into a waiting rowboat. He landed on a pile of bodies belonging to other such unlucky souls. The small boat was silently rowed, under dark of night, to the waiting bark, *Reaper*, which was bound out to sea at daylight. The *Reaper*'s master paid the crimps $50 a body and dumped them into the ship's fo'c'sle or forecastle, a bunkroom in the bow of the ship.

Upon being kicked awake, Sutton found himself on the vomit-crusted deck of the *Reaper*—a beautiful, three-masted wind ship—headed for Australia. The job of the first mate, Bully Hansen, was to manage the crew through sheer brutality. He was known to always kill at least one sailor per voyage to bring the rest of his shanghaied crew into line. After several attempts the first mate could not break the spirit of the burly young logger; so, Hansen broke his skull with an iron belaying pin and tossed the body overboard.

The only unusual aspect of poor John Sutton's story is that somehow the talk got around, and the police were waiting for Hansen when the *Reaper* dropped anchor in San Francisco Bay. More unusual was the fact that Hansen was sent to San Quentin State Prison for the murder.

Another poor Washingtonian met a fate similar to Sutton's, but lived to tell an incredible story. On May 21, 1899,

The *Reaper*   <small>Puget Sound Maritime Historical Society</small>

twenty-one-year-old house painter Charles Walker left his home in Cheney for Spokane. The next thing the young painter knew, he was in a boxcar in Tacoma's railroad yard. In Spokane Walker had been beaten, robbed, and thrown onto a train headed west over the Cascades. While still in the Tacoma freight yards, he met a man who seemed to be looking for work. The stranger offered Walker a meal and a cup of coffee. Though he was grateful for the food, Charles told the stranger that the coffee had a very odd taste; but being broke, hungry, and thirsty, he drank it anyway.

This time when Walker awoke he was aboard the Nova Scotian bark, *Stillwater*. The *Stillwater* was loaded with Northwest timber and already three days out to sea on its journey to South Africa. When Walker protested to the *Stillwater*'s skipper, he was shown his signature on the ship's articles. Insisting he had been shanghaied, he refused to work. Walker changed his mind quickly, however, when he was denied any food until he decided to become part of the crew.

A voyage to East London, South Africa, that should have taken 90 days, took 227, due to uncommonly rough seas. Once in port, the captain told Walker that if he made the return trip he would receive the small salary that, "in my semi-conscious state I had agreed to accept for my service," Walker stated in an interview with a reporter for *The Seattle Times*. Instead he deserted without any pay for the seven and a half months spent at sea.

In South Africa, he enlisted in the British Army. The house painter from Cheney served four years in the army, including two in South Africa's Boer War and one in India patrolling the border. When his enlistment term expired, he joined a survey party in Africa and worked building the railway line from Cape Town to Cairo, Egypt. After that, he shipped to Australia and traveled across China and Japan. Returning to Australia, Walker signed on as a fireman on the White Star Line's steamship *Persic* and stoked fires all the way to England. He traveled across Europe until April 18, 1907, when he left Hamburg, Germany, on a ship bound for Santa Rosalia, Mexico. Back in North America, he worked as a miner and then sailed up the West Coast, eventually landing in Puget Sound on a lumber schooner. Walker finally returned to the Northwest on May 6, 1908. Walker's Oregon City parents had no idea what had become of their son for nine years, until the thirty-year-old finally resurfaced in Washington. Though the excursion took nine years of Walker's life, a Puget Sound crimp on Tacoma's Commencement Bay was paid a price of only $35 for Walker's services.

Could a similar fate have befallen a teenage Harry Long or the multitude of other men listed as missing from the Seattle area?

The practice of shanghaiing that the government had tried to end in 1895 still flourished on Puget Sound in 1905—a fact that was brought to the attention of Seattle's genteel population through a well-publicized incident. On a cold day in late November, witnesses saw three boys dive off of a moving gasoline launch coming up the Sound from Tacoma. One of the boys couldn't swim and was hauled back aboard the ship. The other two swam for the closest shore, Alki Point. The two boys, Archie Cairns and Roy Phelps, were met by curious onlookers on Alki Beach. Their story was that they had been shanghaied in Tacoma and were being taken to the British ship *Scottish Moors*, which was waiting for her crew in Elliott Bay.

The boys then told their tale to Captain Leland of the steamer *Manette*. Leland brought them across Elliott Bay to Seattle and turned them over to government authorities. They were given dry clothes and allowed to stay aboard the United States revenue cutter *Grant*, moored at the foot of King Street, while officers sorted out the facts of their case.

Phelps related his adventure to the police and to Seattle's United States District Attorney Frye. With his two friends, Cairns and Frank Geyer (the third boy who was seen being hauled back onto the boat), Phelps had arrived in Tacoma from San Francisco aboard a lumber schooner several days before the incident. The boys were provided lodging at Tacoma's Sailors' Home. "I am not a sailor," said Phelps, "and I have no desire to go to sea. My home is in New York City, and I wanted to get out into the woods and work for enough money to take me back East." At first the teenagers were treated well, given plenty of food to eat and a warm, dry place to sleep. One morning the boarding house runner told the boys to get their bags and come with him to Seattle. Though they did not want to go, they thought there would be ample opportunity to get away from him when they got to Seattle. The trio was locked in an office for a time before the ship left the Port of Tacoma. There were two other men with them when they boarded the launch. One of the sailors aboard the launch told Phelps and his friends that the British vice consul would come on board the *Scottish Moors* in Seattle and that they would be compelled to sign papers at that time. The sailor went on to say that they would not be allowed to go ashore and there would be no opportunity for them to get ashore before the ship left Elliott Bay.

"Right then and there I decided to get away as soon as possible," said Phelps to a reporter for the *Seattle Post-Intelligencer*, "and I suggested to my friends that we take our chances in the water. We were perhaps a hundred yards from the shore at the time, a mite or two south of Alki Point, and I had no sooner hinted at swimming than Cairns dived overboard. I followed and Geyer came after me. We were in the stern of the launch and I do not think the rest of the fellows on board noticed us when we first went overboard. It was a hard fight in the cold water and when at last I reached a place where I could stand up I was so exhausted that I was unable to wade out for a minute or two. About the time my feet struck bottom I heard Geyer cry out as if frightened and turning around, I saw the men in the launch throw him a line and drag him back on board, but they didn't get Cairns or me."

No sooner had the boys escaped, than the *Scottish Moors* had pulled up anchor and sailed north for Port Townsend with their friend, Geyer, still aboard. When District Attorney Frye was notified of the incident, he contacted federal officers at Port Townsend and instructed them not to allow the *Scottish Moors* to clear Port Townsend until a thorough investigation had been conducted.

Geyer was rescued from the *Scottish Moors* when it reached Port Townsend. The ship's captain and first officer were arrested there and charged with shanghaiing the three young boys. Further investigation showed that twelve of the *Scottish Moor's* crew had jumped ship in Seattle, an indication that perhaps they too had been unwilling sailors.

Although he claimed he was only showing the boys hospitality and they had agreed to work as sailors, the Tacoma boarding house owner and his runner were also charged with attempted abduction. In an ironic twist, a water soaked card advertising the Sailors Home in Old Tacoma was taken from Phelps's pocket. The card's inscription read, "Sailors will find a square house as 'square dealing' is my motto."

Seattle citizens were shocked to learn that a practice, which supposedly ended in 1895, still flourished off their shoreline. "It is disgraceful to think that American citizens should be taken on board foreign vessels in American waters against their wills. Sailor boarding house keepers have been known to be not over scrupulous regarding the methods employed in securing men for ships, and I fear that the incident may prove to be simply an attempt to shanghai three unfortunates," said the captain of the *Grant* in a statement to the *Post-Intelligencer*.

A reporter for *The Seattle Times* wrote, "Why some steps have not been taken in the past two years to break up the gang of crimps operating in Seattle, Tacoma, and Port Townsend is not known. It is a notorious fact that sailors are shanghaied almost every week and the proprietors of the lodging houses are said to receive from $35 to $100 for every man thus furnished them. It is claimed by some government officers that the lodging house men are now working together better than ever before, and that Port Townsend is the headquarters of the 'crimps.'"

The shanghai trade ended around 1911, but not because of any public outcry in response to the stories of kidnapping, brutality, and murder. The trade ended after vessels powered by steam and gasoline engines had replaced the beautiful, wooden, windjammers on the West Coast. It isn't known whether Harry Long's family ever saw him again, or just how many on the lists of missing persons were victims of the shanghai trade.

FLYING SAUCERS OVER MOUNT RAINIER

Before the famous Roswell Incident, there was the Mount Rainier incident. The term "flying saucer," the mysterious "men in black," and conspiracy theories involving the Air Force all originated in the state of Washington.

Around 2:15 p.m. on Tuesday, June 24, 1947, Boise businessman Kenneth Arnold was flying his private plane to Yakima from a business appointment in Chehalis. Arnold owned Great Western Fire Control Supply, a company that sold firefighting equipment, and often flew around the Northwest selling and installing his products. Also a deputy Ada County sheriff and licensed air-rescue pilot, he decided to fly around Mount Rainier to see if he could spot a missing Marine transport plane. A $5,000 reward was being offered to anyone who found the wreck, so it was not unusual for private pilots to circle Mount Rainier in an effort to spot the plane and recover the reward. He searched west-southwest of Rainier for about an hour, and not finding the downed plane, changed course for Yakima. The town of Yakima was approximately 80 miles to the east, and Arnold's plane was 22 miles southwest of Mount Rainier when he switched direction. It was a beautiful summer day with smooth air and crystal clear skies.

He was at an altitude of 9,200 feet when a blinding flash caught his eye. The startled pilot immediately assumed that he was too close to another airplane. In an urgent attempt to locate the other plane, he desperately searched the skies around him. He saw a commercial DC-4 on its San Francisco to Seattle route way off in the distance. Arnold believed a military plane had buzzed him, and he continued to look for it. Then, the blinding flash happened again, but this time he saw the direction it came from— north toward Mount Baker. Looking to the northwest of Mount Rainier, Arnold saw "a chain of nine peculiar looking aircraft flying from north to south at approximately 9,500 feet elevation and going, seemingly, in a definite direction of about 170 degrees." He described their movement as being "like the tail of a Chinese kite, kind of weaving and going at a terrific speed across the face of Mount Rainier." The crafts continued flying at a high rate of speed, with two to three of them dropping and changing direction every few seconds. Each time that happened, there was a flash of light reflecting off the object. Arnold watched as they "flipped and flashed" against the snow in the sunlight "just like a mirror." He wrote, "Another characteristic of these aircraft that made a tremendous impression on me was how they fluttered and sailed, tipping their wings alternately and emitting those very bright blue-white flashes from their surfaces. At the time I did not get the impression that these flashes were emitted by them, but rather that it was the sun's reflection from the extremely highly polished surface of their wings."

Still believing that he was witnessing a formation of military aircraft, Arnold was amazed to note that none of the craft had tails.

Mount Rainier above the clouds   ALAN BAUER PHOTOGRAPHY

The explanation for that, he thought, must be some new form of military camouflage. As the group approached Mount Rainier, it was flying diagonally in echelon formation. The formation reminded Arnold of a flock of Canada geese, flying in a chainlike line.

Arnold noted that he "had never before observed airplanes flying so close to the mountain tops. . . . I was fascinated by this formation of aircraft. They didn't fly like any aircraft I had ever seen before." He turned his plane sideways and opened his window to get a better view.

When he could make out the shapes against the snow-covered slopes of the 14,411-foot mountain, Arnold was able to judge them as being about 50 feet in length and 3 feet thick with a bright metallic finish and no tail. "When the objects were flying approximately straight and level, they were just a black thin line and when they flipped was the only time I could get a judgment as to their size," he said.

By locating landmarks, he estimated the breadth of the formation to be 5 miles across. Judging his distance from the aircraft as 23 miles, the pilot timed the ships as they dipped in and about the craggy Cascade peaks. He noted 102 seconds had passed from the time the objects passed over Mount Rainier to the time they crested Mount Adams to the south. "Even at the time this timing did not upset me as I felt confident after I would land there would be some explanation of what I saw," Arnold recalled.

In his excitement over seeing this bizarre flying formation, Arnold had lost his focus on the $5,000 reward. He thought only of arriving in Yakima so that he could share his experience with other pilots. At the Yakima airport he told a good friend and fellow pilot of the sighting, but the story was jokingly dismissed with his friend telling him he had better change his brand [of liquor]. He then flew to his next destination of Pendleton, Oregon, where he felt he should report his sighting to federal authorities.

After landing in Pendleton, the pilot looked up the distance between Mount Rainier and Mount Adams, found it to be 47 miles, and then calculated the ground speed of the flying disks at upwards of 1,200 miles per hour—more than twice the speed of sound. Arnold discussed the matter with a number of pilots at the Pendleton airfield who did not discount his tale. Retired military pilots told Arnold that they had been briefed during World War II that they might see such anomalies while flying over Europe. One pilot voiced the opinion that the United States or a foreign government was testing a rocket or jet-propelled ship.

The next day in town, Arnold first tried to report his findings to the local Federal Bureau of Investigation office because he thought that the flying objects might have been Russian. The FBI office was closed, so he went to the *East Oregonian* newspaper office with his story. In describing the sight to newspaper column editor Nolan Skiff and reporter Bill Bequette, he stated, "The objects flew like a saucer would if you skipped it across the water." Bequette later said of the meeting, "Both Nolan Skiff and I were in the office, which was small, when Mr. Arnold came in. As I remember, we both talked with him, listened to his story, told him we didn't have a clue to what he had seen but would send the story to the Associated Press in hopes some editor or newspaper reader might be able to explain the strange objects." The interview only lasted about five minutes.

Skiff made some notes and then wrote a short article, which they squeezed into the bottom of the *East Oregonian*'s front page. Bequette then punched in an abbreviated version to the AP wire. The wire was dispatched late on the morning of June 25, 1947. When he returned from lunch break after the wire had gone out, he was greeted by an astounded receptionist who told him that newspapers from all over the country had been calling for more information about the "flying saucers." Northwest newspapers printed the AP report the evening of June 25, and by June 26 the story had spread across the continent.

Now the young reporter knew he had a story. Bequette interviewed Ken Arnold at his hotel for two hours and then wrote a 40 column inch story for Portland's Associated Press Bureau. The article was published on page one of nearly every newspaper in the nation. Both Bequette and Skiff had been impressed by Arnold's sincere, honest demeanor. They did not think he was someone who "saw things." Rather, they believed Arnold seemed genuinely puzzled by what he had witnessed.

Once the story was out, many theories were presented. Were the aircraft U.S. or Soviet secret weapons? The Air Force immediately informed the press that it was not responsible for the flying saucers, nor was it developing any such secret weapon. Air Force Command suggested sun reflections off of clouds, meteors breaking up against the snowy peaks, or hailstones were the cause.

Within two days of Arnold's sighting, after the news story had been printed across the United States, other witnesses came forward with similar stories. Fred Johnson was prospecting in the Cascade range near Mount Adams on June 24, 1947, the same day as Arnold's event, when his attention was drawn to the sky by a brilliant reflection. He saw a disk-shaped object flying in a southeastern direction. Through his telescope, Johnson watched five to six flying craft pass overhead. He concentrated on one disk for about forty-five to sixty seconds. Johnson watched as the craft banked in the sun. He estimated the formation was about 1,000 feet above his altitude of 5,000 feet. He judged each disk to be 30 feet in diameter. They made no sound as they flew. Immediately before the fleet flew over, the needle on Johnson's compass began to jerk about erratically. After they had passed by, the compass operated normally.

Johnson continued prospecting in the Cascade range for several more days before he returned to his home in Portland where he read the article about Arnold's sighting of the same day.

Kenneth Arnold in the plane he was piloting when he spotted UFOs over Mount Rainier KENNETH ARNOLD, *THE COMING OF THE SAUCERS*, 1952.

He also read that the military authorities had stated they had no knowledge of any such occurrence. Johnson contacted the Army–Air Force with the intent of adding credibility to Arnold's story. Johnson's report to the military was listed in *Project Blue Book* as the first of 700 unexplained sightings the report contained.

Project Blue Book was compiled by Air Force investigators at the Air Technical Intelligence Center at Wright-Patterson Air Force Base in Dayton, Ohio. In an attempt to give the public conventional explanations for the great number of sightings, Air Force investigators compiled 13,000 reported sightings between 1947 and 1969. Of that number 700 were not explained because "there was not enough information to allow a positive identification."

The analysts mistakenly separated Arnold and Johnson's sightings and reported them as two different events. Johnson's account fell into the "unexplained" category after he'd been interviewed by military intelligence officers on three different occasions. Arnold's story was said to have inconsistencies and was deemed a "mirage."

Even though Arnold's vision was dismissed in *Project Blue Book*, as Washington state native and legendary journalist Edward R. Murrow reported after a 1950 interview with Arnold, "While Mr. Arnold's original explanation has been forgotten, the term 'flying saucer' has become a household word."

During July 1947, witnesses also told of seeing flying objects over Bremerton, Bellingham, Spokane, and Yakima. A Eugene, Oregon, resident produced a photograph of saucers flying in formation. A laboratory analysis concluded the spots were dust on the negative. Another UFO photo was taken by Seattle resident Frank Ryman and published in the *Seattle Post-Intelligencer* on July 5, 1947.

On July 4, several hundred people claimed they saw shiny, flying saucers traveling at high rates of speed over Portland. That same evening, as United Flight 105 was in the sky over Idaho, Captain E. J. Smith witnessed a formation of five flying disks joined by four more several minutes later. Smith's copilot confirmed the sight; then, the two called the flight attendant into the cockpit. She exclaimed, "Why, there's a formation of those flying disks!" The trio watched the formation for about ten minutes before it sped out of sight. The following day, Captain Smith contacted Arnold about his adventure. The two would combine forces and continue to investigate mysterious Northwest UFO sightings for many years.

Publication of the many witness accounts had been made from coast to coast when on July 8, 1947, the wreckage of an alleged flying saucer was reported in Roswell, New Mexico. The Roswell event was to overshadow the Rainier UFOs over time.

More than a month after Arnold's encounter, he and Captain Smith met with two Puget Sound marine-salvage boat operators who claimed to have found the wreckage of a UFO on a Maury Island beach on June 21, 1947. Harold Dahl was boating off Maury Island between Seattle and Tacoma with his teenage son, their dog, and two crewmen. He claimed to have seen six "shell-like gold and silver color," "doughnut-shaped" flying objects, one of which seemed to be in trouble. The troubled craft appeared to spew metallic material, then the boaters heard a loud thud, like an underground explosion. He said that his boat was damaged, his son's arm injured, and the dog killed by falling debris. The boat's radio was rendered useless during the event. Dahl also said he took photographs of the scene.

Upon returning to shore, Dahl told his boss, Fred Crisman, of the incident. Angry over the damage to his vessel, Crisman went to Maury Island to investigate. He discovered a large amount of metal and rock debris scattered across the beach. Pilots Arnold and Smith met with Dahl and Crisman in late July. They examined the beach debris, which appeared to them to be lavalike rock and aluminum aircraft scraps. By then, the photos had disappeared.

Dahl told the two that a mysterious stranger in a black suit had driven up to him in a 1947 Buick and had warned him not to relate his story to anyone if he cared for his family's welfare. Arnold and Smith called Lieutenant Frank M. Brown and

Captain William L. Davidson of Air Force intelligence to investigate. The two officers flew up from Hamilton Field in California. After interviewing Dahl and Crisman and seeing samples of the UFO wreckage, the investigators suddenly lost all interest in pursuing the matter. Brown and Davidson claimed that their plane was being called back to Hamilton Field to take part in maneuvers for Air Force Day. According to Arnold, "Captain Smith and I thought their excuse for getting back to Hamilton Field was rather flimsy. . . Even though they were as polite and nice as you could ask, they gave me the impression they thought Smith and I were the victims of some silly hoax." Before leaving McChord Air Force Base on August 1, 1947, Brown and Davidson told the base's intelligence officer of the "hoax."

The plane never returned to California. It burst into flames and crashed near Kelso, killing Lieutenant Brown and Captain Davidson, but sparing two crewmen. "Sabotage Hinted In Crash of Army Bomber At Kelso: Plane May Hold Flying Disk Secret" blared the headline printed in red ink. The *Tacoma Times* reported the crash as suspicious and wrote that the plane was carrying "classified material," when it had been "shot down" to prevent further analysis of the UFO wreckage. Further investigation revealed Crisman and Dahl as frauds who had invented the UFO incident to profit from the sale of the story to a magazine. The Maury Island event, though exposed as a total hoax, gave birth to the myth of the mysterious black-clad government agents and military conspiracy theories.

The crash of another Air Force plane on April 1, 1959, added to the mystery. While flying east of the Pierce County town of Sumner, the pilot radioed that he had hit, or been hit, by something. Witnesses saw the plane as it passed overhead, its engines dead and glowing, round disks trailing in its wake. The entire crew of four was killed in the crash.

There were 850 sightings of UFOs reported during 1947, most of them coming after Arnold's story was published. Throughout World War II, citizens were told to be vigilant in watching the skies and to report anything unusual to authorities. After World War II, the public experienced great anxiety over the advent of atomic weapons, followed by an atmosphere of distrust of the Soviets that prevailed during the Cold War era. These historical realities may have increased the phenomena of UFO experiences. Upholding their civic duty, people were watching the skies more, and Ken Arnold's experience encouraged witnesses to report sightings and gave a name to previously unidentifiable observations—"flying saucers."

Though flying saucer events were well publicized in 1947, there was also a wave of sightings from 1896 through 1897. The *Tacoma Daily Ledger* printed an article about a sighting by a Tacoma couple on November 27, 1896. When Mrs. St. John noticed an unusual light through her bedroom window, she pointed it out to her husband. The couple described seeing a brilliant light traveling at a high rate of speed just to the east of Mount Tacoma (an Indian name for Mount Rainier). They watched as the object flew south, flashing colored rays of light in all directions as it moved. The light swayed back and forth "like a vessel at sea in a storm." Mr. St. John surmised that they had possibly witnessed an "airship," as he had recently read of one being developed in California.

Are UFOs drawn to the towering majesty of Mount Rainier? Local tribes were in awe of the mountain and its power. Sluiskin, a Yakama-Klickitat Indian who guided Hazard Stevens and Philemon Van Trump, the first men to summit the mountain in 1870, refused to climb above the snow line due to his awe and reverence of the mountain's spirit. Perhaps the danger, mystery, and power of the ancient volcano is as much a draw to otherworldly visitors as it has always been to those who live in view of the majestic peak.

THE MAD DOCTOR'S SOUTH HILL MANSION

Mysterious shadows creeping across the walls and strange, unexplained, noises have been reported by the mansion's caretakers. Previous owners swear they have seen the apparition of a woman at the top of the stairway. Neighborhood children dare each other to run up and touch the haunted house. Rumors abound about screams coming from within its walls. The home's occupants have reportedly heard either angry, arguing voices or sounds of laughing frivolity. Some even speak of bloodstains appearing and disappearing on the floors of the old South Hill mansion.

The floors of Spokane's most infamous haunted house have indeed been drenched in blood during its history. Shootings, suicide, electroshock treatments, and illegal operations, performed by a man Spokane's press dubbed The Mad Doctor, all occurred inside the walls of the stately old residence. Secret tunnels, buried treasure, death, and mayhem are all part of the mansion's aura.

The history of the Wilbur-Hahn manor began in September 1916 with the marriage of Sarah (Hecla) Smith, widow and heir to a fortune made in the Hecla Silver Mine, to Ralston T. "Jack" Wilbur. Using Sarah's money, Jack hired a noted architect to build an elaborate, craftsman-style home for his new bride, who was sixteen years his senior. The three-story, seventeen-room house cost

$75,000 to build and boasted imported marble, gold-leaf carvings, high-beamed ceilings, and mahogany paneling inlaid with mother of pearl shipped from China. It sat on nearly four acres of land on Spokane's fashionable South Hill. The new Mrs. Wilbur reportedly was not overly impressed with the new home or its neighborhood, causing a rift in the couple's relationship. They divorced in 1918, and the home was sold to druggist William T. Whitlock.

In 1924, the most notorious resident, Rudolph A. Hahn, purchased the house. Hahn moved into the residence with his second wife, Sylvia, who was thirty-two years younger than he was. The couple spent $50,000 on improvements, including a swimming pool and lush gardens decorated with elaborate fountains and ornate statues. Secret wall panels and passageways were built inside the house, perhaps to hide the doctor's illegal activities.

Never legitimately licensed as a physician, Hahn was a former barber and portrait painter who earned his fortune by providing electroshock therapy to cure the ills of his wealthy clients. Electrotherapy came into fashion in the early twentieth century as a quick, push-button manner of diagnosing and curing all sorts of diseases, including cancer. From as little as one drop of blood, an electrotherapist would "diagnose" a malady and then prescribe shock treatments as a cure. These "doctors" could make $2,000 per week with such treatments. Hidden income came from the secret abortions that Hahn quietly performed in his basement for upper-class Inland Empire patients. Many people in Spokane believed that Hahn buried much of his illegally obtained fortune on his property. A legend grew about thousands of dollars in gold that had been hidden by "Dr." Hahn.

The "doctor" had a love of expensive, fast cars and boats, which he sometimes raced. His multiple-car garage usually stored at least two extravagant, stylish automobiles. When his fancy turned to racehorses, the mansion's front lawn served as a pasture where he kept the sleek steeds grazing.

Hahn Manor became a famous venue for extravagant parties. Even during Prohibition, raucous events with free-flowing alcohol were the rule. During one such event, Hahn drove his car into the swimming pool. The pool was then filled with dirt to prevent further such episodes.

The infamous parties often hosted celebrities of the day including flying ace Jimmie Doolittle, who became famous during World War II with his Doolittle's Raiders. Doolittle was known to dive his plane at the home during events, much to the delight of the eccentric "doctor."

Always a fan of boisterous entertainment and the newest innovations, Hahn built a radio tower in his yard and installed enormous speakers so that he could listen to his radio from anywhere on his four-acre grounds. Much to the dismay of his neighbors, the broadcasts from these loudspeakers could be heard for miles around, so they went to court and obtained an injunction to silence them.

Later that same year, in October 1929, Hahn was again in court, this time charged with performing an illegal abortion on a high-school girl from Idaho. The allegation included charges that the girl had nearly died as a result of the operation. Hahn claimed he had seen the girl for stomach pains only and had asked her to return to the home for a blood test. By his own admission, the "doctor" had received his medical diploma and license to practice through a correspondence course. Hahn admitted he had been a barber who studied x-ray and specialized in "electrotherapeutics." A jury acquitted him of the crime, finding insufficient evidence to convict.

The energy of the mansion seemed a detriment to matrimony both for the four-times married Sarah Hecla Smith Wilbur and for the Hahns. The Hahns filed for divorce three times. On the occasion that Sylvia filed for dissolution in 1932, she claimed her husband was abusing her. At trial, she testified that her spouse had threatened to run her through with a sword and had chased her out of the house while brandishing the weapon. By 1933, however, the couple had remarried stating that keeping in touch by telephone was much too expensive. Just two months later, in August 1933, Hahn appeared in police court with broken ribs. Both husband and wife were charged with drunken and disorderly behavior. Sylvia Hahn admitted guilt in causing her husband's injuries and was given a fifteen-day, suspended sentence. The doctor was found not culpable. Before 1934 was over, Hahn had filed for divorce and reconciled with his wife yet again.

On May 2, 1940, Hahn was arrested for questioning in the death of his young wife, Sylvia. According to Hahn, he had been outside on the porch when he heard a gunshot. Upon rushing into his wife's bedroom, he found Sylvia lying on a blood-soaked bed with a Luger in her hand and a bullet hole through her right ear. When police arrived, they found racehorses grazing on the front lawn and a very drunk Hahn on the premises. Sylvia's lifeless body lay in a bedroom that was riddled with bullet holes, and the lock had been shot off of the bedroom door. Due to the many prior

Front view of the Hahn Mansion on Spokane's South Hill   THE *SPOKESMAN-REVIEW*

abuse allegations and the fact that Hahn was known to have threatened his wife with guns from his collection and to have taken target
practice inside the house, Hahn was interrogated. After several days
a coroner's jury concluded that Sylvia had died from a wound she,
herself, inflicted and Hahn was released from jail.

Only five years had passed since his wife's death when Hahn
was arrested again. This time he was charged with manslaughter
and three counts of performing illegal abortions in his home.
The wife of a wealthy eastern Washington farmer had died as a
result of one of Hahn's abortions. The manslaughter charge was
dropped, but a jury found the doctor guilty on two counts of abortion at trial in June 1945. Defense attorneys argued that a prison
sentence would ensure certain death for the eighty-year-old Hahn.
The judge clearly stated his belief that Hahn had been operating

on women within the walls of his home for years and he saw no reason for clemency. He did agree, however, that the law did not provide for the death penalty in such cases and prison would be a death sentence for the frail, old "doctor." Hahn's sentence was commuted to probation and a $1,000 fine, if he promised never to practice medicine again. The "good doctor" agreed and instructed the prosecutor to donate his operating table, electroshock equipment and surgical instruments to Gonzaga University. That same year, saying he could no longer live in his home with pleasure, Hahn sold the South Hill home.

Hahn was living in a downtown Spokane hotel when his son found him on the floor of his apartment with a 2-foot, antique, French bayonet through his heart. A three-carat diamond had been pried from the doctor's tiepin, his wallet was bare, and an empty sheath for the bayonet lay near the body. The blood-spattered room had been torn apart, and it was evident that a violent struggle had ensued. The bayonet used to murder Rudolph Hahn, August 6, 1946, was from his own collection of antique weapons. A Federal Bureau of Investigation manhunt for Hahn's killer resulted in the arrest of an ex-convict named Delbert "Frenchy" Visger, who admitted he killed the elderly man during a robbery.

The Wilbur-Hahn Mansion was eventually purchased by Spokane County to be used as a retirement home. After that, it lay abandoned and in disrepair for years before recent buyers took turns renovating the old home. A lawyer, who owned the house throughout the eighties told of being approached by many people who asked permission to search the grounds with metal detectors for the treasure they believed Hahn had buried there. Nothing of the ill-gotten fortune was ever found.

The house, with its mysterious hidden passageways, rumors of buried treasure, and ghostly sightings, is now on the Spokane Register of Historic Places. The Hahns' legacy of excess with their lavish parties, drunken brawls, gun and sword play, brutal shock treatments, bloody operations, suicide, and death surely have left a unique, dark aura about the storied estate.

In 1991, a group of college-student ghost hunters staying overnight in the house reported hearing all kinds of inexplicable noises and the distinct sound of a woman crying several times during the night. At one point, witnesses saw the mysterious black form of some strange creature appear in a window. Members of the ghost-hunting party described the active presence of spirits in the old manor. Perhaps the energy of the home's eccentric previous occupants remains with the historic mansion.

STRANGE STEILACOOM

On a recent Halloween night members of a local ghost-hunting group convened at Fort Steilacoom Park. The ghost hunters hoped to detect otherworldly presences at the site of a graveyard and former working farm belonging to the state's oldest mental institution, Western State Hospital, formerly known as Washington State Hospital for the Insane. Much suffering occurred at the old hospital. In addition to being the home of hundreds of tortured souls, it was the site of many experimental surgeries, including frontal lobotomies in the early twentieth century.

Over 3,000 former inhabitants of the Washington State Hospital for the Insane were buried in the cemetery between 1876 and 1953. Most of the graves were merely marked with small stones etched with the patients' identification numbers. Before being deeded to the state for "use as an insane asylum," the grounds housed Fort Steilacoom, a place built for trade, for protection, and for meting out frontier justice.

Under a full moon, the ghost-hunting party searched through crumbling gravestones and abandoned buildings. Suddenly an electromagnetic field reading picked up great spikes of energy. Swirls of foglike wisps hung low to the earth, curling around the spooky old remnants of buildings and graves. A psychic felt the presence of an angry spirit who wanted them to leave. Later, photographs of the ghost hunt showed ectoplasm, or thin veils of fog, that the professional photographer never saw.

Steilacoom, Washington's oldest incorporated town, has long had a reputation for being haunted. Fort Steilacoom was the site of the first capital trial and official hanging in the Puget Sound region. The fort was also the prison for Chief Leschi, an innocent man wrongly accused of the wartime killing of a soldier. He was later hanged from a scaffold built on grounds nearby.

During the Civil War Fort Steilacoom was deserted and became "an insane asylum," where great suffering and hideous operations took place. Several houses, the site of the old mental hospital and graveyard, and the woods around Fort Steilacoom have all been the scenes of strange occurrences. Ghost hunters frequently search for psychic energy, ectoplasms, and unearthly sounds and sights there.

Under the light of the moon, the ghost of J. M. Bates has been seen wandering around Steilacoom searching for his lost cow. Bates was a poor man of limited intelligence who had one prized possession, his cow. When the animal disappeared one day in 1863, a distraught Bates went looking for the cow all around town. In search of answers, Bates began questioning patrons of Steilacoom's saloons. A man who had been imbibing in one of the bars told Bates that he had seen the cow's head impaled on a pike at Andrew Byrd's slaughterhouse. Byrd was a prosperous South Sound citizen who owned a gristmill, a sawmill, and a slaughter-house all located in the Chambers Creek Estuary. Byrd was so prominent that the first officially recognized road in Washington, the Byrd Mill Road (now Steilacoom Boulevard) was named after him. Whether the man in the saloon had a vendetta against Byrd or he was just having fun with the slow-witted Bates isn't clear, but the information provided was false. Nevertheless Bates believed it and set out looking for the wealthy miller.

An agitated Bates found Byrd and confronted him about the missing cow. Byrd told Bates that he had nothing to do with the cow's disappearance and that he should go away and look elsewhere for the missing bovine. He even suggested that Bates check his slaughterhouse if he didn't believe him. Bates did leave but his anger intensified, fueled by the false information fed to him. Bates made threats against Byrd over the next few days, but no one took him seriously until January 21, 1863.

Byrd was known to go to Steilacoom's post office when he came to town. Knowing Byrd's routine, Bates lay in wait for three days, and when Byrd came to town, Bates shot him twice, once in the torso and once in the leg. He chased the wounded victim into the street in an attempt to shoot him a third time before horrified bystanders stopped him.

Bates was arrested and thrown into the local jail as the fatally wounded Byrd lingered on for another day. Before he died, Byrd defended his shooter saying, "Don't do anything to that man. He's a little retarded." The night of Byrd's death, up to 150 of Steilacoom's residents broke into the jail using a battering ram, sledgehammers, axes, and crowbars to force the door off its hinges. The group detained the sheriff and removed Bates from his cell. A rope was thrown around his neck, and the murderer was dragged to a barn where the mob lynched him. The body was left hanging from a pole outside the barn for the entire day.

Thinking he might be next, the saloon patron who had identified Byrd as the cow thief left town suddenly and headed south for the Oregon border.

Apparitions of J. M. Bates with a noose around his neck, dragging a lead rope behind him have been seen in the woods near Steilacoom Lake and in town near the old jail or saloons. It appears when a bright moon shines above to light the way for Bates, who is said to be still searching for his missing cow.

Not all of Steilacoom's ghosts wander the streets and forests. Some remain in the homes and businesses that they once loved. The ghost of E. R. Rogers in his rocking chair has been seen through an upstairs window in the grand mansion he had built on Commercial Street in 1891. Bells ringing and mysterious thumping sounds from above have all been experienced in the mansion-turned-restaurant. A customer in the restaurant's bar once saw a woman's shoeless foot walking through the air as if ascending invisible stairs into the attic. Staff members who have gone into the attic have suddenly been saturated in the smell of heavy perfume permeating the room. Electrical problems, including small appliances that switch on and off for no reason, have become fairly common in the dining and bar areas.

Once a bartender turned off the lights and locked up the building upon leaving, only to look back and see someone inside with the lights on. He called the police who brought a K-9 officer with them to search the establishment. Finding no one inside the restaurant or on the lower floors, the officers ordered the dog to check the attic. The K-9 refused to go upstairs although he had always been obedient before. Night cleaning crews have also quit unexpectedly giving no other explanation than that they believed the mansion was haunted.

A disembodied face has been seen in the branches of a tree on the corner of the yard. Stories tell of a local Indian man who was hanged from the tree's limbs. The mysterious visage appears to shine from the branches in the darkness of night.

Edwin R. Rogers, a merchant and mariner, built the mansion overlooking Puget Sound during prosperous times for his wife, Catherine, and daughter, Kate. Unfortunately, they only lived there two years before a financial crisis during the crash of 1893 forced his family out. They moved next door to the modest house they had once occupied.

The next occupants of the Rogers mansion were the Herman family, who operated a bed-and-breakfast in the mansion. Charles Herman and his wife rented rooms out to summer vacationers.

The Bair family, who ran a drug and hardware store they built on Lafayette Street in 1895, bought the Roger's mansion in 1920. W. L. Bair and his wife, Hattie, rented rooms to boarders through World War II, while running their drugstore, soda fountain, hardware store, and post office in the next block. Hattie was known for her hospitable spirit. She always had food and a room for down-on-their-luck men passing through, which she provided in exchange for chores. The Bair store became a post office and trolley station run by daughter, Eudocia, after her father's death. In the 1970s the Bair family bequeathed their store to the Steilacoom Historical Museum Association, which today operates it as a restaurant/museum.

However, W. L. Bair never left his drugstore, even after death. Strange phenomena continue to be experienced there, and

Western Washington Hospital for the Insane, Steilacoom, ca. 1913, now known as Western State Hospital UNIVERSITY OF WASHINGTON LIBRARIES, SPECIAL COLLECTIONS, UW 23920

Bair's image has even been captured in photographs of the old business. Appliances in the restaurant became unexpectedly temperamental as soon as the restaurant began operation. Kitchen utensils would disappear, only to show up across the store in unusual places. Most everyone who has worked at the restaurant has heard a woman's voice calling their names when no one else is present. Patrons and wait staff alike once witnessed a bottle of sauce come flying off of the shelf for no apparent reason, except that "someone" didn't like the new product being sold in the store. The proprietors blame the unexplained phenomenon on W. L. Bair, who was known to be reluctant to embrace any type of change. His spirit seems to rebel against new appliances or products introduced into his establishment.

Strange happenings are nothing new in the town of Steila-coom. The brother of town founder, Lafayette Balch, died under mysterious circumstances, and his body was discovered half-naked in the woods with an ax tightly gripped in one hand. A passerby discovered the man's body lying near the road that ran between Steilacoom and Olympia. The body had no obvious wounds. Local authorities could only piece together what had happened to Albert G. Balch.

During a fierce Northwest winter windstorm, on December 27, 1862, Albert Balch must have been startled awake by the violent storm and jumped from his bed. Grabbing an ax for protection, he took off running through the woods. He ran through the thick forest for hours by moonlight before his fatal collapse. Perhaps he fainted from exhaustion, maybe he hit his head, or his life was extinguished by exposure to the elements.

Balch suffered periodic bouts of "insanity" which his family and neighbors associated with the moon's cycle. His neighbors were terrified by his erratic behavior. Once during a full moon, Balch, who had gone to San Francisco to purchase goods for his store, was found aimlessly wandering the California city's streets late at night with $2,500 in gold in his briefcase.

It was well known in the Washington Territory that Balch's episodes were brought about by a full moon. During his last known affliction, he expressed paranoia and talked about his enemies chasing him and wanting to harm or kill him. His death was never fully explained.

Washington's oldest port, first incorporated town, and home to the state's first "insane asylum" seems to be a haven for a disproportionate number of unearthly spirits. One historian, who also heads up ghost tours through town, believes fourteen sites within the town of Steilacoom are haunted by ghosts. Steilacoom remains a draw for ghost hunters from all over Washington.

THE EARL OF BLEWETT PASS

Freddie and Billy Burmeister, two teenage Chelan County boys, were hunting on the mountainside above the small mining town of Blewett on a clear, sunny, late-winter day in 1905. As they trudged over the snow-covered ground, they noticed the light from a lantern shining through the window of the strange hermit's cabin. The boys could not resist peeking through the recluse's grimy window. The sight within made them take off running down the slippery slope in terror.

There, on the bed, lay the still, stiff body of the lonely miner. His wide-open eyes stared back at the two faces peering in the window. The boys had just decided that old Tom Douglas was dead and they should go notify someone; when, suddenly, the glassy eyes blinked. Billy and Freddie turned and ran for town.

Bursting into the Blewett Post Office they exclaimed to Postmaster Henry Resberg, "Douglas is laying in his bunk. He's dead except for just his eyes and they're alive. He saw us and blinked them!"

Resberg, who was also justice of the peace, contacted the Chelan County prosecutor for authority to go into the reclusive prospector's cabin and investigate the matter. Upon entering the hermit's hut, Resberg found Douglas still lying on his bed completely paralyzed. Douglas had suffered a stroke, and judging by the amount of oil left in his burning lantern, he had been laying there, helpless, for two to three days.

Under the care of Mrs. Resberg, Douglas lived in that state for several more days. When he died on March 18, 1905, he was buried in the town's small, hillside cemetery. But who was Tom Douglas?

The Scotsman had appeared in Blewett some time in the 1890s. The town of Blewett, on Blewett Pass, was formed around 1860, after miners, returning from the Fraser River gold rush, discovered rich placer claims in the area. Accessible at first only by rugged mountain trails, then by a crude wagon road from Cle Elum, it had a population of 200 to 300—mostly miners—by the time Douglas appeared on the scene.

Douglas staked a claim that he named The Jupiter and worked at prospecting when it suited him. He didn't seem to need the money, and he paid in cash for everything he bought—usually liquor. The eccentric Scot was moody and unsociable and kept almost entirely to himself. He was known to spend his days inside his home, reading and drinking alone. The enormous volume of Douglas's many newspaper and magazine subscriptions drove postmaster Resberg crazy—especially when the subscriber would disappear for weeks at a time. Every now and then, Douglas left Blewett for Leavenworth and boarded a train for some unknown destination. No one ever knew where he went or why. He never left a trail like most townsfolk by riding the triweekly stage or catching a ride out of town with the team drivers for one of the mining company wagons.

Douglas did have one friend, another Scot named J. A. "Archie" McKinnon. In 1900, Frank Reeves was running for prosecuting attorney of the newly formed Chelan County and had come to Blewett to court the miners' votes. The miners declared the day a holiday in order to attend Reeves's party at the Blewett Saloon and indulge in the free drinks provided. The saloon was filled with 200 miners, drinking and dancing to fiddle and guitar music, when McKinnon and Douglas rode into camp. Since they had been prospecting at The Jupiter for a few days, they hadn't gotten the word about the big party. Though they were dirty, bearded, and tired from trekking down from the mountains, the noise from the saloon drew their interest. With Douglas trailing behind him, McKinnon led his packhorse, which was still fully loaded with their gear, directly into the saloon. Complete with animal and equipment, the two then walked right up to the bar to order their drinks. For a moment the entire room fell silent as the revelers stared at the crusty duo and their packhorse. Shrugging off the bizarre entrance, the party continued with the fiddling, singing, and dancing. The men had not had time to order a drink when there was a deafening crack, the building shuddered violently, and the floorboards suddenly gave way. The horse, men, and bar fell into the basement of the saloon. Not missing a beat, the town fiddler located his fiddle in the rubble and struck up a tune, "Captain Jinks of the Horse Marines," as the men and horse crawled out of the cellar. The party was moved to the schoolhouse, and a bar was set up in a classroom. Reeves gave his campaign speech and after the town's women joined the affair, there was dancing until dawn. Reeves was elected Chelan County's first prosecuting attorney.

Douglas was also known to host the occasional card game. He sometimes invited other odd, older bachelors, like himself, to his small cabin to play poker. He had just returned from one of his mysterious

Town of Blewett, ca. 1890   USDA Forest Service

---

trips when he had "the boys" in for a poker game. Douglas had been drinking heavily that night when he announced to his guests in his heavy brogue, "This is too tame. I want some excitement."

With that, he rummaged around and slid a large, metal box out from under his bunk. When Douglas popped open the lid, his guests could not believe what they saw. The box was full to the top with gold coins. Using a pile of coins to gamble, the group played cards into the night. When Douglas had his fill of cards, he picked up the coins, carefully counted them, placed them back into the cash box, and sent his guests home.

Rumors spread around town about the Scotsman's hoard of gold. Now Blewett's citizens knew how Douglas could have an endless supply of cash when his mining claim, The Jupiter, was virtually worthless. In fact, Douglas sold "one whole and undivided interest" in The Jupiter to Archie McKinnon on May 1, 1902, for $1. Still nobody bothered the recluse. The code of the Blewett Mining District was "Mind your own business." Then, there was the fact that Douglas was known to keep a loaded six-shooter by his side at all times.

Still, the old man must have regretted revealing his secret cache. Shortly after the revelation, he was seen burying a chest on his property. His closest neighbors were a family who lived about 300 yards away. Late one fall night, the mother was up tending to a sick child when a bouncing light caught her eye. Through her window she saw what at first appeared to be a glow, "like that of a lightning bug," coming from just behind Tom Douglas's cabin. She could just make out the form of a man digging a hole, with the outline of a rectangular box on the ground beside him. The dutiful mother shrugged it off and turned her attention back to nursing her ailing child.

Henry Resberg was once again becoming annoyed with the tall stack of newspapers and magazines that were piling up at the post office, since Douglas had not come in to pick them up for several days, when the Burmeister boys rushed in with the news of finding Tom in his cabin. The Resbergs' attempts to nurse the invalid miner back to health having failed, Henry Resberg immediately contacted Reeves for advice on dealing with Douglas's effects. Reeves deemed the matter "an emergency," and a court hearing was held on the very day of Douglas's death. Reeves advised the court, "The deceased has a cabin at Blewett with some personal effects therein, and that same are liable to be carried away or

destroyed if some person does not have authority to take imme-
diate charge thereof." Perhaps Reeves and Resberg worried that
town gold hunters might tear apart Douglas's property. A commis-
sioner ruled "That Thomas Douglas died intestate in the County
of Chelan, State of Washington, on the 18th day of March, 1905,
leaving an estate in the County of Chelan, State of Washington,
that it is necessary in order to preserve said estate that some competent person be appointed to take charge of said estate and of the
effects of the said Thomas Douglas, deceased." Resberg was then
appointed temporary administrator of Thomas Douglas's estate
and ordered to inventory the estate and to make a written report
to the court within thirty days.

With his court-appointed authority, Resberg entered the
Douglas cabin to prepare an inventory of the estate and to determine whether the mysterious old Scotsman had any heirs. Henry
found Douglas's work clothes and some papers, but no cache of
gold coins. Douglas's treasures consisted of a scrap of yellowed
paper, part of a letter inscribed, "With all my love, Jenny." There
was also an 1850 birth certificate from Perth, Scotland, for
Thomas Douglas, son of James and Mary Douglas.

Resberg wrote to the postmaster for Perth, Scotland, in
an attempt to notify the Douglas family of Tom's death. Three
months later a letter arrived from a law firm in Scotland. The
letter informed Resberg that Douglas's parents, James and Mary
Douglas, had been the Earl and Countess of Angus. Tom was their
eldest son and heir to the Scottish title.

The Douglas family is among Scotland's most noble clans.
The *Imperial Gazetteer of Scotland* notes, "The family was raised to

an earldom in 1357, by David II; and during this reign and the two which succeeded, the house of Douglas rose to a degree of power scarcely inferior to that of royalty itself; so that, as has been remarked by an old historian, it became a saying that 'nae man was safe in the country, unless he were either a Douglas or a Douglas man.'"

While in his twenties, Tom Douglas had become estranged from his father, the Earl, when he had secretly married a girl from the village—a commoner—without his family's approval. Tom vowed he would never set foot in the Douglas ancestral home again. He and his bride then sailed for America in the mid 1870s.

Not much was known about the couple before Douglas surfaced on Blewett Pass. It was rumored that his wife had died, and that they had been the parents of three children, some who were still living in Seattle. More than five years after Douglas's death, his attorney had only been able to determine "that so far as your petitioner has ever been able to ascertain the heirs of Thomas Douglas, deceased, are a daughter, who is now probably twenty-three or twenty-four years old, and a son who is probably eighteen or nineteen years old, and whose addresses are unknown at the present time to your petitioner, but the last known address was Seattle and Tacoma, respectively." It is not known if the heirs were ever located and informed of their father's death.

Tales of Tom Douglas's peerage flooded Chelan County. The story of Douglas burying a chest in the middle of the night took on new life. The soft, spring-thawed ground around the Douglas cabin was thoroughly excavated by many of the town's prospectors. No box of gold coins was ever found.

MADCAP MAY'S CURSE

Seattle entertainment magnate John Considine, known as Boss Sport, got the shock of his life when he saw the toast of four continents scrubbing floors at Seattle North Pacific Shipyards. He was stunned to encounter the actress-singer May Yohe, whom he had booked to open Seattle's elegant Coliseum Theater in 1907, cleaning offices on Seattle's waterfront.

Considine was visiting the shipyard offices one fall day in 1918 when he discovered the former star. Clearly no one at the shipyards knew her identity. Seattle North Pacific employees were shocked to hear the following exchange:

"My god, Mayse, is this a farce comedy or what?" he exclaimed loudly.

"It's what," May replied, shaking out her dust rag.

Considine, who had once paid the actress $1,000 a week to perform at The Coliseum, then turned and announced to all at the shipyard, "Do you know who this is?" His question was met with heavy silence from a wide-eyed audience, so he answered it himself, "She is the Lady Francis Hope—May Yohe."

The woman, who had performed on the light opera stages of America and London, told a newspaper reporter that the only difference the discovery made to the men at the shipyards, who had already been very good to her, was to make them even kinder and more considerate.

May's unfortunate circumstances might have been just another riches-to-rags story or the tale of a stage career gone wrong, but May blamed her bad luck on a curse—the curse of the Hope Diamond. As she told a reporter for Seattle's *Post-Intelligencer* in 1918, "Mayse of the stage, Mayse of the Hope Diamond and newspaper scandals is gone." The former Madcap May insisted that Mary Ann was now going to live a quiet life.

No references to a curse on the Hope Diamond are known to have existed before 1909, when the *London Times* carried a fanciful article written by Paris correspondent George Saunders after the gem had changed hands at a Paris auction. Five months later, *The New York Times* reported that the seller, "a wealthy Turkish diamond collector and merchant," named Salomon Habib, had perished in a shipwreck and implied that he had met his end as a result of dealing with the diamond. The American public became captivated with the legend and its ties to American actress May Yohe. The curse of the Hope Diamond was largely formed, propagated, and publicized through the exploits of May Yohe with the tale taking on new life when the national and world press learned that the former darling of the stage and ex-wife of the English Lord Francis Hope had been found scouring shipyard office floors in Seattle.

Mary Augusta Yohe was born to William Yohe, former Army officer and proprietor of the Eagle Hotel in Bethlehem, Pennsylvania, and Lizzie Yohe, a Narragansett Indian descendant, on April 6, 1869. Lizzie sent her daughter to Europe at the age of

The former Lady Francis Hope, May Yohe, 1909

twelve to be politely educated. Her first stage job was as a chorus girl, but success as an actress came in 1887 with a production in Chicago. May and her deep, peculiar, contralto voice were especially popular in London. She was a favorite of Edward, Prince of Wales. A prized possession in her one-room Seattle apartment was a sterling-silver-framed photo of King Edward VII inscribed, "To May, 1898." Though she captured the fascination of the future King of England, she married an English lord, Sir Henry Francis Hope Pelham-Clinton Hope, on November 27, 1894. Hope was the younger brother of the Duke of Manchester, heir to the title Duke of Newcastle, and owner of the Hope Diamond, which he had inherited as part of a life trust from his grandmother.

The enormous, 45.52-carat, sapphire-blue diamond, allegedly stolen originally from a Hindu idol and later from the French crown during the revolution, came into the Hope family when Henry Philip Hope purchased it for $90,000 in 1830. "Philip" Hope gave the stone the name by which it is still known today. After several generations Lord Francis Hope inherited the diamond. A notorious gambler and playboy, Hope went into bankruptcy a year after marrying the American actress. *Life* magazine stated in a 1938 piece that Lord Francis gave his bride the Hope Diamond as a wedding present; but, May claimed that she only wore the diamond twice— once in 1894 at her wedding party and again in 1900 at a party given in London to welcome the Hopes home from New York. Lord Hope attempted to sell the gem in 1898, but the request was denied by trustees administering to his fortune, by his siblings, and by the courts. Madcap May, beloved actress of the English stage, supported the couple through financial difficulties.

In 1900, while Lord Francis and Lady May Hope were in New York, May became enamored with Major Putnam Bradlee Strong, a former Army officer, hero of the Spanish-American War, and son of the one-time mayor of New York City. Major Strong and Lady May ran off to Japan in April 1901. Later that year Lord Francis was finally allowed by the English courts to sell the Hope Diamond. The famous jewel left the Hope family in the fall of 1901. Lord and Lady Hope were granted a divorce in March 1902. By April Lord Francis was again bankrupt and had suffered a leg amputation after accidentally shooting himself.

Lady Hope and Major Strong traveled the world and married in Buenos Aires as soon as her divorce was final in 1902. The couple lived a lavish lifestyle until their money began to run out. The suave, gallant, but womanizing Strong began to pawn and sell May's jewelry to pay off debts until one day when he emptied out her safe-deposit box with another woman at his side. According to May, Strong had deserted her in New York just three years into the marriage, but the Strongs separated and reconciled several times. By 1910, May was living in a second-rate rooming house in Seattle "with meager fortune." Strong was penniless in Macao, China, while May stayed in the Northwest. A *Post-Intelligencer* article reported, "As May Yohe, Mrs. Strong again attempted vaudeville, but her old-time success was gone, charm was gone, and her engagements were short. The woman who wore the stone and brought disgrace upon a peer of England has been lying ill with a fever in Portland."

In 1910, Mrs. Putnam Bradlee Strong filed for dissolution in Oregon City and in her divorce complaint blamed much of her misfortune on the curse of the Hope Diamond. This fueled reports in Northwest newspapers such as, "Murder, sudden death, lies, deceit and treachery have followed in the wake of the great Hope Diamond which the complainant in this Oregon divorce case flaunted from the vaudeville stage a few years ago." The actress blamed her circumstances on the glamorous gem and perpetuated the myth that the diamond had been stolen from the altar of a Hindu temple in India by Jean Tavernier, as well as the myth that Tavernier was torn to bits by wild dogs just a few years later. She attributed the executions of Louis XVI and Marie Antoinette, as well as many other deaths and disgraces, including Lord Hope's and her own fall from wealth and grace, to the famous diamond.

Though she wore the Hope Diamond only twice, May used the infamous indigo stone to enhance her own star status for the rest of her life. She attempted a comeback on the London stage in 1912, wearing a replica of the Hope Diamond. Lord Francis, who had a box seat for the performance, was said to have been moved to tears by the sight of his ex-wife wearing a copy of the family jewel.

While performing in South Africa, May met Captain John "Jack" Smuts—barrister and former South African Army officer—whom she married in 1914. The Smutses moved to Singapore, where Captain Smuts managed a large oil company. Next, they lived on a plantation in Jahore, Bahru, Malaysia, under the patronage of the sultan. The couple traveled extensively throughout the Far East and resided in India, China, and Japan. When World War I broke out in 1917, Captain Smuts tried to reenlist, but a hammertoe prevented him from serving. With military service not an option, the couple left Japan in 1918 with much of their holdings depleted.

In desperate need of money, May gave concerts in San Francisco and Portland. When they arrived in Seattle, May received word of her mother's death. Lizzie Yohe had gone to work as a seamstress to support her daughter's musical training in Europe after her husband died. Though Lizzie passed away while her daughter was in Japan, word did not get to May until she reached Seattle.

"I could not sing with that news on my heart. I knew that if I appeared on the Coast and made a failure that people would say May Yohe was dead and that I would lose the sweet taste of other triumphs. I wanted to leave the stage with the memory of success."

Smuts found a position in the machine shops at the Seattle North Pacific Shipyards, and they settled in Seattle. Their home was a small one-room flat at the El Rey Apartments at 2119 Second Avenue in downtown Seattle. The woman who had once owned great European art masterpieces now decorated the walls of her tiny rooming-house abode with pictures from a 15-cent store. Smuts's foot injury and the influenza, which swept the world in 1918, rendered him unable to work.

May went to the shipyards to obtain Jack's paycheck after he had fallen ill. At the Seattle North Pacific yards, she ran into the company physician who had attended her husband. The doctor jokingly asked her if she were there looking for a position. To his shock she asked if he knew of one. After referring her to the employment window, the doctor vouched for her and helped her obtain the janitress job. When Smuts learned she had taken the position, he immediately dressed and went to his job on the docks. The exertion caused a severe relapse of his illness, which nearly killed him.

She had been employed at the Seattle shipyard a little more than a week when Considine discovered her there, broom in hand. The event became worldwide news and added fuel to the tales of the legendary curse. Near the end of the storied actress's life, a 1938 *Life* magazine article stated that "she worked as a scrubwoman, housekeeper and janitress." These were probably all references to May's job at the Seattle shipyards. When interviewed about working as a janitress, she told the press that she and Smuts planned to settle on a small parcel of land north of the city, raise chickens, and, "wait for the haze of this last adventure in May Yohe's career to clear away." She claimed that she was done with the stage, though Smuts insisted she was not.

The Smutses' marriage may not have been as blissful as May portrayed when she stated that Jack was the only man who had brought her true happiness. Her husband suffered a mysterious gunshot wound to the chest in 1924. A suicide note, written in an unfamiliar hand, was found stating that he had shot himself because he had been unkind to his wife. Smuts recovered and no charges resulted from the shooting. The Smutses' marriage, no matter the faults, lasted another fourteen years until May's death.

The chicken farm, like most of the Smutses' endeavors, including The Blue Diamond Inn (which burned to the ground one year after it was built in New Hampshire), was not successful. After the failure of each business, May returned to performing always wearing the replica of the Hope Diamond.

In an attempt to revive her acting career, May capitalized on her association with the diamond further by writing and starring in a Hollywood film serial entitled *The Hope Diamond Mystery*.

The 1921 series of films, featuring Boris Karloff, included fifteen episodes of mostly fictional characters who had suffered great tragedies as a result of their association with the midnight-blue stone.

When the films were not successful, May contacted writer H. L. Gates and enticed him to write *The Mystery of the Hope Diamond*, published in 1921. Gates's book was advertised as being told from "the personal narrative of Lady Francis Hope (May Yohe). . . . [about] that sinister crystal which has wrecked so many lives and still deals death and destruction to all who come beneath its influence."

The book begins with "French Soldier," Jean Tavernier, desecrating a temple in Burma and stealing the beautiful blue stone from an idol in 1588. Tavernier dies a terrible death in Russia when he is torn apart by wild dogs just a few years after stealing the stone.

Jean-Baptiste Tavernier was actually an honorable French merchant who was born in 1605, seventeen years after May claimed that he stole the diamond. After purchasing the 112-carat diamond in India (not Burma), Tavernier sold the diamond, then known as the Tavernier Blue, to Louis XIV, "The Sun King," in 1668. Louis XIV recut the diamond to sixty-seven and one-eighth carats and named it "The Blue Diamond of the Crown," more commonly known as "The French Blue." Though it is not certain how the jewel merchant died in Russia, he was eighty-four years old at the time of his death in 1689.

The Mystery of the Hope Diamond contained many exotic scenes and situations, some based on historical figures and others completely fictionalized. Authors Gates and Yohe introduced their readers to the following collection of characters and myths:

Louis XIV's minister of finance, Nicholas Fouquet, borrowed the gem to wear at a ball and was executed by the Sun King the following day. In fact, there was a royal ball like the one portrayed, but it was held nearly eight years before the king purchased the Tavernier stone. Fouquet was imprisoned the day after the grand ball, but he was not executed.

Madame de Montespan, the king's favorite mistress, was given the diamond by her lover, who promptly abandoned her and cast her from his court. Historically, de Montespan was rumored to have participated in a Black Mass and have been involved in poisoning her enemies. The king never thought her guilty, but became more enamored with another woman and evicted her from her quarters seventeen years after she first became his lover.

The Sun King himself died in disgrace of an agonizing death as a result of owning the Tavernier Blue. Actually, his three-week-long illness and agonizing death were due to gangrene. France was still a major world power when Louis XIV died, though it had suffered economic and military problems.

Princess de Lamballe, a friend of Marie Antoinette, wore the diamond and was then ripped limb from limb by a French mob during the French Revolution. The beautiful princess probably never wore the diamond, as it had been set in the Order of the Golden Fleece for the king the year the princess was born. The diamond was in this mounting, intended to be worn only by Louis XVI, from 1749 until it was stolen in 1792. Princess de Lamballe was, indeed, torn apart at the hands of an angry French mob.

King Louis XVI and Marie Antoinette died on the guillotine as a result of inheriting the stone. Since the French Blue had been set in the Order of the Golden Fleece, it is not likely that Marie Antoinette actually wore the diamond. The French royal couple were beheaded on the guillotine during the French Revolution.

French revolutionary leader Jean-Paul Marat stole the royal diamond from the French court in 1792 and was killed in a gruesome manner while bathing. Marat was not a member of the gang of thieves who stole the diamond from the French court. Though he was murdered in his bathtub, many bloody killings occurred during the French Revolution.

The Dutch diamond cutter Wilhelm Fals, who is reported as the one who re-cut the diamond to its present forty-four and a-half carats, died of grief when his son, Hendrik, stole the French Blue from him. Hendrik took the gem from Amsterdam to London, where he committed suicide in 1830. In fact the blue diamond was probably taken to England by Cadet Guillot, one of the thieves who robbed the French royal family. It is not clear if there was a Dutch diamond cutter involved or if these people existed at all. No one knows where the stolen stone was cut, how, or by whom.

Francois Beaulieu came to possess the French Blue as the result of its owner's suicide. Desperate for money, Beaulieu sold the diamond to Englishman Daniel Eliason for much less than it was worth and then died of starvation the day after the sale. Nothing is known of Beaulieu, and Eliason never spoke of the diamond's history, possibly because he knew it had been stolen from France. Drawings of the blue diamond surfaced in London in 1812, twenty years and two days after it had been stolen from the French crown jewels. Under French law a statute of limitations provided amnesty after twenty years for all crimes committed during war.

The Hope family obtained the stone from Eliason and had very public financial losses, scandal, embarrassment, and tragedy as a result. Lord Francis Hope's financial difficulties were largely brought about by his own gambling and affluent lifestyle. Lord Francis did endure embarrassment and heartbreak when his wife, May Yohe, ran off with another man, and he did shoot his leg off. Though he may have suffered financial, physical, and emotional injury, Lord Francis remarried, had three children, and became the Duke of Newcastle at the age of sixty-two.

Additional characters in May Yohe's farce were: Jacques Colot, a diamond dealer, who brokered a sale of the diamond and then went insane and committed suicide; actress Lorens Ladue, who was shot to death on stage while wearing the Hope Diamond, which her lover, Russian Prince Kanitovsky, had provided her; the shooter, Prince Kanitovsky, who died within days of the murder of stab wounds inflicted by Russian revolutionaries; a Greek jeweler, Simon Montharides, who sold the diamond to the Sultan of Turkey, then died with his entire family in a car accident; and Jehver Agha of the Turkish court, who attempted to steal the stone from the sultan and was hanged for his efforts. Evidence that any of these people or events occurred is sparse or nonexistent.

Even before the book release or movie premiere, Madcap May's adventures cultivated the mystery of the Hope Diamond's curse, and a savvy salesman, Pierre Cartier, exploited the stories when he sold the stone to mining heiress Evalyn Walsh McLean in 1912. The legends intrigued the new owner who wore the deep, blue gem with flair. When she learned of the sale, May wrote the first of many letters to McLean warning her of the bad luck that she had endured as a result of owning the Hope Diamond. In her book, *Father Struck It Rich*, McLean describes May writing to her: "As one woman to another she begged me to throw it away and break its spell." McLean attributed the correspondence as an attempt by Yohe to "recoup some bit of happiness from the ruin of her life." McLean's life was far from perfect, though, as she suffered her own misfortune with the death of her nine-year-old son in an auto accident, the sleeping pill overdose of her twenty-five-year old daughter, the institutionalization of her philandering husband in a mental hospital, and her own morphine use. Following McLean's death, the stone was purchased by noted New York jeweler Harry Winston, who donated it to the Smithsonian Institution in 1958.

May Yohe-Hope Strong Smuts died of a heart attack in Boston on August 28, 1938, at the age of sixty-nine. Though she traded on her association with the Hope Diamond to the very end, it was the discovery of the famous stage actress working as a janitress in Seattle that greatly publicized her misfortune and fall from grace and captured the fascination of the American public. While Madcap May Yohe is largely forgotten and her life in the Northwest mostly unknown, the attention this onetime Seattle shipyard scrubwoman brought to the "curse" of the Hope Diamond makes the Hope Diamond a renowned icon to this day.

KENNEWICK MAN

T
he two college students waded into the Columbia River looking for free entry into the Tri-Cities' biggest summer event, the hydroplane races on the Columbia River. About 10 feet from the river's bank, Will Thomas's foot hit something round lodged in the riverbed. He turned to his friend, Dave Deacy, and joked that he had found a human head. Reaching underwater he felt something like a large rock and pulled it from the river. Examining the brown, mud-caked object, the young man noticed teeth and realized he really was holding a human skull.

Not wanting to miss the final heat of the hydro races, the two hid the skull in some bushes along the shore. When the race ended, they returned with a bucket to retrieve the find. They dumped the mud-covered skull upside down into the bucket and proceeded to look for a policeman among the many who were working crowd control at Columbia Park in Kennewick that summer day of July 28, 1996.

Thinking they had a murder on their hands, Kennewick police officers and Benton County Sheriff's deputies took the boys by patrol boat to the site to see the exact location of their discovery. The investigators found more bone fragments in the river and on the shore. That evening Columbia Basin Dive Rescue Team members were called in to help investigate the crime scene.

They planned to map and tape off the area so they could sift for evidence. The skull was sent to the crime lab for examination.

Upon initial examination, Benton County officials realized the skull was very old and had been buried for many years. Based on the skull's shape and facial bones, which appeared Caucasian, the coroner assumed it belonged to an early pioneer of European descent.

The Benton County coroner called in Richland anthropologist and consultant James Chatters for further evaluation. Chatters returned to the site of the find and was able to excavate a nearly complete skeleton from underneath 3 feet of compacted earth and sand. Based on the shape of the skull, Chatters also believed the remains were those of a person of European descent, so he was surprised to find an ancient stone-chiseled spear point embedded in the skeleton's pelvis. The ancient projectile was not something one would have expected to find lodged in a nineteenth-century settler's hip bone. Chatters sent a sample of bone to the University of California at Riverside for carbon dating. The results could not have been more stunning. They showed that the man found in the Columbia River had lived in the area sometime between 7565 BC and 7235 BC.

Soon after the announcement of the discovery of a 9,500-year-old skeleton, both excitement and controversy erupted. Scientists across the country became fascinated with the find, so old, yet so different from what they would expect to find with an ancient American Indian skull. Fewer than twelve skulls older than 8,000 years had ever been discovered on the American continents. This skeleton, named Kennewick Man, was one of the oldest, most complete skeletons ever found in the Americas.

Older bone fragments had been discovered in the Northwest. Cremated bones of a person who had lived in Washington 10,000 to 11,000 years earlier were found in 1968 at Marmes rock shelter. The excavation was cut off after only a few months, when a flood of water from the Snake River's Lower Monumental Dam covered the site.

The complete skeleton of a twenty-year-old woman, dated at 10,675 years old, had been discovered near Buhl, Idaho, in 1992. Before a thorough study could be made, though, the skeleton was given to the Shoshone-Bannock Tribes for burial.

Representatives of the Umatilla and Colville Confederated Tribes claimed Kennewick Man as an ancestor and demanded the bones be returned to them for burial pursuant to The Native American Graves Protection and Repatriation Act (NAGPRA). The 1990 federal law had been enacted to end the wanton destruction of gravesites and the thoughtless collecting of American Indian remains for souvenirs, sale, or study. American Indian bones were to be returned to indigenous tribes for respectful burial.

Before the skeleton could be shipped to the Smithsonian Institution for in-depth research, the Army Corps of Engineers seized it. The fate of Kennewick Man then lay with the Corps of Engineers. Though leased and managed as a park by the City of Kennewick, the land where the skeleton was discovered was owned by the Corps, which had jurisdiction over the remains. Lieutenant Colonel Donald Curtis Jr., the Corps's Walla Walla District engineer, waited until late October 1996 to see what claims would be made on Kennewick Man. The Confederated Tribes of the Umatilla Indian Reservation, Confederated Tribes of the Colville Reservation, Confederated Tribes and Bands of the Yakama Indian

Nation, Nez Perce Tribe of Idaho, and the Wanapum Band came forward to claim the bones. Since oral histories stated that their ancestors had been part of the land since the dawn of time and had not migrated, the tribes believed the bones to be The Ancient One as told by their history. These Northwest tribes believed that the study of the remains amounted to desecration of a grave and was an affront to their very beliefs. They wanted to return the bones to the ground so the spirit of The Ancient One could be at peace. The Army Corps of Engineers decided to return the bones of Kennewick Man to the tribes for reburial.

A group of scientists filed suit to stop the burial. Both the National Park Service (NAGPRA administrator) and U.S. Secretary of the Interior, Bruce Babbitt, intervened on behalf of the tribes. The Corps of Engineers turned the bones over to the Secretary of the Interior; and in April 1998 the Corps buried the site of the original discovery under two million pounds of soil and gravel. Though the Corps claimed the action was needed to stabilize eroding shorelines and save migrating salmon, covering the area prevented any further excavating or the involvement of the Corps in future controversy. The action of the Corps effectively ended all efforts to determine whether other artifacts were present at the site.

Years of litigation followed. Anthropologists argued that the bones were too old and dissimilar to be traced to any Northwest tribes of today; therefore, Kennewick Man was not their ancestor. Kennewick Man's skull was long with a narrow face and cheekbones, a prominent nose and chin similar to the populations of South Asia. American Indians tended to have features more similar to those found in North Asia—wider, flatter faces and rounded skulls.

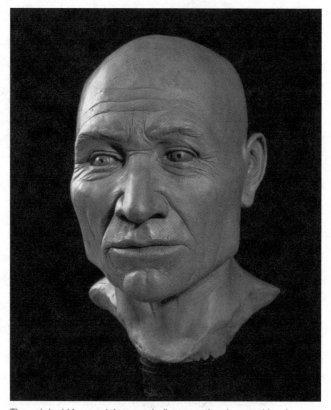

The original Kennewick man skull re-creation (created by James Chatters and Tom McClelland) JAMES CHATTERS

A federal judge ordered the bones be moved to the Burke Museum at the University of Washington as a neutral repository until the dispute could be resolved. In 1999 a team of scientists was allowed to begin study of the remains in order to determine clues to his origin. Many theories of his origin were presented. His skull, teeth and bone measurements were compared to 300 known racial and ethnic populations and did not match any of them. The scientists showed that cranial measurements and features of the skull most closely resembled those of Polynesians and South Asians and were significantly different than those of any Indian tribe currently living in North America. Due to the age and condition of the bones, no DNA could be found or extracted for testing.

Anthropologists date the beginnings of the Columbia Plateau tribal culture to 2,000 to 3,000 years ago. They believe that shelters, diet, subsistence patterns, style of tools and weapons, and burial rituals were substantially different from Kennewick Man's time. No villages or settlements were believed to have existed on the Columbia Plateau over 9,000 years ago, when human populations were small, nomadic groups traveling long distances for food and materials. They theorize that it was not until 2,000 to 3,000 years ago that populations began to settle into villages and bands related to existing tribes. Scientists argued that today's tribes' oral histories could be from a culture very different from the one to which Kennewick Man belonged. The courts observed that 8,340 to 9,200 years between Kennewick Man's life and present day tribes was too long a time to bridge with oral tradition alone.

Common belief held that the ancestors of American Indians crossed a land bridge over the Bering Sea from Asia to North America in one mass migration. There are inconsistencies in that theory such as the number of different languages in the Pacific Northwest, the differences in features between Eastern and Western American Indians, and the fact that American tools seem to be designed like those found in Europe rather than in Asia.

Were there multiple groups of humans who crossed the Bering Sea land bridge from different places and in different eras? Did the first Americans cross the Pacific in boats? A Polynesian man came forth in 2001 to stake a claim to Kennewick Man by filing to intervene in the federal case. Some anthropologists believe the first Americans could have come from Europe via Iceland and Greenland when the sea levels were much lower. The Asatru Folk Assembly, a group practicing pre-Christian, European religion later followed by the Vikings, conducted ceremonies in Columbia Park on August 27, 1997, and stated their belief that Kennewick Man was their early European ancestor.

So, who were Kennewick Man and his people—the first Washingtonians—who hunted and lived on the Columbia Plateau up to 9,500 years ago? This was a time predating all recorded history. The bones have told us that he looked different than today's American Indians. His skull was longer and less round, and he was relatively tall. He stood about 5 feet, 9 inches tall and was thirty-five to fifty-five years of age at the time of his death. As a teenager he had suffered an attack by a human enemy. A spear had been thrown with such force that it had entered the back of the hip and embedded itself in his bone. The attack had not killed the teen, though; bone grew around the stone point as he aged. At some time in his life, he had also suffered a crushed rib cage and a withered arm. Still, he walked erect, did not limp, and suffered no arthritis. After his death the body was immediately buried before scavengers could get to it. The dead man's body could have been covered by a natural event like a flood, or his tribesmen may have buried him.

Was Kennewick Man part of a much earlier migration than the one that brought descendants of today's Northwest tribes to the area? Did his people die out or intermarry with a later group?

Will further study answer questions about the earliest inhabitants of Washington and America and will it even be allowed? On February 4, 2004, the Ninth Circuit Court of Appeals ruled that the plaintiffs, scientists, could continue to study the remains of Kennewick Man. The court held, "Because Kennewick Man's remains are so old and the information about his era is so limited, the record does not permit the Secretary [of the Interior] to conclude reasonably that Kennewick Man shares special and significant genetic or cultural features with presently existing indigenous tribes, people, or cultures. We thus hold that Kennewick Man's remains are not Native American human remains within the meaning of NAGPRA. . . . Studies of the Kennewick Man's remains by Plaintiffs-scientists may proceed."

After the Ninth Circuit Court of Appeals remanded the case to the U.S. District Court for the District of Oregon, U.S. Magistrate Judge John Jelderks ruled on August 17, 2004, that any further legal action be limited to anthropologists studying Kennewick Man and to government agencies. This decision effectively bars Northwest Indian tribes from participating as a party in any further lawsuits. The tribes are attempting to intervene in the case and seeking to show that their "oral traditions and beliefs" are enough to show a cultural link to Kennewick Man, giving them a protectable interest in seeing that the remains and their burial site are respectfully studied, curated, and reinterred.

Kennewick Man may yet find himself before the United States Supreme Court or Congress before this dispute is resolved. The mystery of Kennewick Man may never be solved, although modern science is bringing us closer to a conclusion than ever before.

Scientists were allowed to more thoroughly examine and study Kennewick Man in 2005, after the court's final determination. Led by anthropologist Doug Owsley of the Smithsonian Institution, they were able to study isotopes from the bones, which showed the man's diet had consisted of marine animals. This finding led them to deduce that he had probably lived on the coast rather than along the Columbia River. Thus, Owsley believed he was not related to the Inland-Area tribes who claimed him as an ancestor. When told of this finding in 2012, Columbia Plateau–area tribal members disagreed, stating that their ancestors would have eaten lamprey (an eel-like fish), accounting for the finding. The plateau tribes still firmly believe "The Ancient One" is their ancestor, and they plan to ask Congress to change the NAGPRA law so that they may one day bury the remains.

In 2007, divers in the Gulf of Mexico discovered the skeleton of a young girl with features very similar to those of Kennewick Man. Genetic testing done on DNA extracted from one of her teeth showed that though her physical features were different from today's Native Americans, she shared genetic traits and was their ancestor. Some archaeologists believed this proved that differences in appearance between the skulls belonging to the girl and Kennewick Man, versus those of modern Native Americans, must be due to evolution rather than genetics. In fact, further analysis of Kennewick Man's skull has resulted in a new facial reconstruction of the Ancient One, which differs markedly from the more Caucasian model first published.

The technology of DNA extraction and genetic analysis has advanced exponentially over the decades since Kennewick Man was discovered. While DNA recovery was not successful (or even permitted) in the 1990s, scientists have now been able to extract DNA from the bones. Genome sequencing and analysis was done at the world's leading facility at the University of Copenhagen. The results of the gene sequencing study, published June 18, 2015, show that Kennewick Man is the genetic ancestor of today's Native Americans and is related to Inland Northwest tribes.

HEXED

Alll of you who have had anything to do with my case will be punished. I am putting the Jake Bird hex on you. Mark my words, you will die before I do!" exclaimed the defendant.

The judge pounded his gavel, "That'll be enough, Mr. Bird. You've had your say. Now, I will have mine. On January 16, 1948, at precisely one minute past midnight, I sentence you to be hung by the neck until dead. The sentence will be carried out at the Washington State Penitentiary, Walla Walla."

With that, one of the country's most prolific serial killers was sentenced to hang for two of his murders. But the sentence was not without consequences. In January, the very same month that he had sentenced the defendant to be hung, the trial court judge died unexpectedly. Before the year 1948 had ended, five of the men involved in Bird's incarceration and prosecution were gone. A sixth man, one of the guards at the state prison, died two months before the execution took place. Had they all died as a result of the killer's hex? Or was the hex merely a hoax, meant to frighten those who had pursued and imprisoned the mass murderer?

The early hours of October 30, 1947, the day before Halloween, were dark and damp as an evil presence stalked the citizens of Tacoma looking for his prey. That rainy Northwest night, a transient railroad worker broke into the Tacoma home of a middle-aged widow and her teenaged daughter and hacked both of them to death with an ax. The itinerant laborer had arrived in Tacoma three days earlier. By his own admission, he had walked from his hotel into a residential neighborhood looking for a house that would be easy to rob. His routine was to prowl a neighborhood, find an open door, and enter a home armed with a pipe, knife, or ax. Once inside, he would listen for movement, and then take off his shoes to ensure that his victims would never hear him coming. On this night, he decided on a house on Twenty-first Street, grabbed an ax from a shed in the backyard, and entered the premises through an unlocked back door. He took off his shoes and left them near his escape route. A woman was sleeping in a bedroom next to the kitchen as he approached. The intruder grabbed her purse from the dresser. In his confession, he claimed that the older woman awoke and began screaming. When her daughter heard her mother's cries she came running downstairs. According to the burglar, the two women attempted to overpower him, and he swung his ax at them as they fought with him. The women were cut and bludgeoned repeatedly until both were dead from the vicious ax attack.

As he left the home, the killer noticed a police car approaching. The two officers had been alerted to the crime when a neighbor reported hearing screams coming from the house. Officer Evan "Skip" Davies and Andrew "Tiny" Sabutis approached the front and back porches just as a shadowy figure darted around the side of the house. Davies, a former football tackle, chased the man through backyards and over fences for nearly two blocks before cornering him behind some bushes in an alley. Revolver drawn,

Davies commanded the suspect to come out and show himself. The man rushed from his hiding place, charging at the officer. He cursed, screamed, and stabbed at Davies, "fighting back like a madman." The attacker slashed Davies's hand as the policeman clubbed him to the ground with his gun and called for his partner. Now laying on the ground, but still fighting his arrest, the killer stabbed Officer Sabutis in the back as he tried to restrain him with handcuffs. The officers finally subdued the knife-wielding man with several punches and kicks to the groin.

All three men were taken to Tacoma hospitals for their injuries. Sabutis was hospitalized for several days; Davies, once his hand was treated, returned to the crime scene with another officer. The perpetrator was taken to the prison ward of Pierce County Hospital.

Although it was early morning, the skies were still dark and drizzly as the officers approached the home where the murders had taken place. When they entered the house, they found young Beverly Kludt's body lying in a dining nook between the kitchen and the bedroom hallway. Her mother, Bertha, was lying in her bedroom. Both women had been brutally beaten and repeatedly stabbed. The rooms were awash in blood, and it looked like there had been a violent struggle as the women fought for their lives.

By morning, the medical examiner had inspected the prisoner's clothing and soon determined that the blood saturating them belonged to Mrs. Kludt and her daughter. The suspect's pants were streaked gray with brain matter, thought to be from blows to the mother's head. Fingerprints belonging to the prisoner were

View of the back porch and rear entrance to the Kludt home, where the serial killer entered and exited   Courtesy Tacoma Public Library

found in the home and on the ax left at the murder scene. Within hours of his arrest, the killer had issued a one-page, recorded confession.

Bruised, battered, and covered in blood when taken into custody, the balding, black male stood six feet tall and weighed 185 pounds. The prisoner was identified as a forty-five-year-old transient, originally from Louisiana. He left home before he was twenty to join a roving carnival and had spent his life constantly on the move, taking odd jobs and wandering the country. By unraveling the details of his life, investigators learned that Jake Bird had also left a trail of murder in his wake as he traveled from state to state.

As news of the crime spread, investigators from around the United States came to Tacoma seeking answers to unsolved homicides in their cities. Police departments from Houston, Chicago, Los Angeles, and New York contacted the Tacoma Police Department about Bird. Pierce County investigators discovered that Bird had served prison time in Utah, Iowa, and Michigan for violent assaults and robberies. Many of his victims had been attacked with axes or hatchets. Since most of the victims were women, some authorities suspected that the perpetrator's motives may have been of a more deviant nature.

Bird had worked as a laborer on the railroad, continuously moving around the country from job to job. When he came to a new town, his habit was to walk around a neighborhood near the railroad tracks, peeking into windows, and looking for women living alone. On his last night in a town, the itinerant laborer would enter a home to rob and assault the residents. He always removed his shoes and took an ax or club with him. After beating or slashing the people inside, he ransacked the home. The killer was cold and calculating, but never remorseful. When asked if Jake was capable of being remorseful, one witness answered, "Killing was second nature to him. He snuffed out human life the way you'd mash a fly."

Far from the ignorant, illiterate he was first thought to be, Bird impressed his interviewers as intelligent, gregarious, and well-mannered when it suited him. He was a man who had educated himself in prison libraries and often defended himself in court proceedings. An investigator spoke of his impressions saying, "Jake was a very fascinating fellow, dangerous as sin, but fascinating."

Jake Bird was tried for murder in Pierce County Superior Court. Even though he had signed a confession within hours of the crime, he now pled innocence, claiming that the confession had been beaten out of him. It took the jury thirty-five minutes to reach their verdict: two counts of first degree murder. Eleven days later, at his sentencing before the judge, Bird still feigned innocence. That failing, he glared menacingly into the faces around him and proclaimed his hex upon them all.

Authorities transported the condemned man across the state to the penitentiary at Walla Walla the day after sentencing. As the Pierce County sheriff drove him to prison, the shackled man talked about his involvement in multiple murders. Once at the prison, Bird immediately began to bargain for his life. He sent word to the warden telling him that if he was appointed a lawyer to appeal his case and stay his execution, he could help "clear up" ten unsolved murders, maybe more. The Pierce County prosecuting attorney and a Tacoma police detective were sent to Walla Walla to hear the confessions. Jake Bird was given a sixty-day reprieve by the governor after he had implicated himself in as many as forty-four slayings nationwide. The governor was wary of the prisoner's tactics, saying, "A stay of execution may be granted to clean up other murders. However, if we see that the confessions are lies, we will not grant any delays."

Bird claimed knowledge of killings in twelve states over a twenty-year period. He was tied to victims in Colorado, Florida, Illinois, Indiana, Iowa, Kansas, Kentucky, Nebraska, Ohio, South Dakota, Utah, and Wisconsin. Of the nearly fifty slayings he was suspected of, eleven were ultimately proven to have been committed by the serial killer.

Was Jake Bird the most prolific serial murderer of his time? Though only eleven of the crimes could be definitively tied to Bird, he was certainly a person of interest, suspected of involvement in at least forty-four other unsolved homicides committed from coast to coast.

The first of multiple appeals was filed January 12 with the Washington State Supreme Court. Jake appeared as his own attorney at several hearings. He argued that his confession had been beaten out of him, that he had not received proper counsel, and, that as a black man who had been the subject of sensational press, he could not have received a fair trial in Pierce County. Before it was over, the Bird case had been heard by the Washington Supreme Court three times, and it had been appealed to both the United States Court of Appeals and the United States Supreme Court. When his last appeal to the U.S. Supreme Court had been denied and the governor refused to grant any more reprieves, Bird was sentenced to hang. Jake Bird was hanged on July 15, 1949, and buried in the prison cemetery in a grave marked only with his inmate number.

Before his execution was carried out, six men associated with the serial killer's trial and incarceration had dropped dead. Five of the deaths had occurred within one year of the original murder trial. The sixth died just before Bird was hung.

The first to go was the judge who had presided over the state's murder case and had sentenced Jake Bird to be executed. The judge died abruptly within a month of sentencing the defendant to hang.

Soon after, a Pierce County Superior Court Clerk involved with the trial had died.

The sheriff who had transported the prisoner across Washington to the state penitentiary and had heard him confess to multiple murders committed over a twenty-year span was dead at the age of forty-six.

A Tacoma police detective who had investigated, interviewed, and listened to Bird's prison confessions died within six months of the trial, also at the age of forty-six.

Tacoma newspaper headlines read, "Fifth Man in Bird's 'Hex' Dies," after one of Bird's own defense attorneys keeled over at his desk while reading legal briefs. Bird had accused the court-appointed attorney of providing him with an inadequate defense at trial. Defendant Bird told an appellate judge that his own lawyer had said his life "should be obliterated." The record does show that during the trial, the defense attorney had actually told the jury, "My heart does not beat in sympathy for this man who fixed his life as more important than that of others."

Those who had been in the courtroom that day began to wonder if they would be the next to go. Was the hex real? Could it take them too?

The sixth to suffer a fatal ailment was one of Bird's death row prison guards at the Walla Walla penitentiary. The guard was taken by an acute illness two months prior to the hanging.

Were these men cursed by some Bayou black magic that Jake had learned in his native state?

Had their deaths been brought about by the serial killer's courtroom hex?

All of the men died of heart conditions or severe, unforeseen illness; but did the hex bring about these previously undiagnosed afflictions? Not everyone in the courtroom that day suffered a fatal event. Still, it seems a strange coincidence that so many involved with the killer shared the very same fate.

YACOLT—VALLEY OF EVIL SPIRITS

The children set out that day to fill their baskets with succulent berries as was their Klickitat tribal tradition. They were headed to a lush valley, surrounded by dark, forbidding woods where the berries were known to be plentiful. Huckleberries, blueberries, and even strawberries grew in abundance on this prairie. When the children did not return to their village that night, their elders went looking for them, but the entire group of children had vanished. No trace of the berry pickers was ever found. Members of the Klickitat Tribe believed that dark spirits had lured the children into the forest and devoured them. The Klickitats named the area "Yalicolb," meaning Haunted Place or Valley of Evil Spirits.

This eerie valley, nestled near the foothills of the Cascade Mountains between Mount St. Helens and the Columbia Gorge, has long been a place steeped in mystery and great tragedy. Residents of the small town of Yacolt, named for the Klickitat "Yalicolb," still talk of hearing the sounds of children laughing and playing when none are there. The owner of a local restaurant located in an old building tells of being awakened at night by strange sounds emanating from her back stairway. Occasionally, she also hears children laughing, though there are none living there. Another resident claims to have seen the ghostly vision of a black-haired woman in a mirror. The valley and surrounding forests are said to harbor ghosts, evil spirits, demons, and beasts. The area has been the site of wars, plagues, and one of the largest forest fires in Washington state history.

Some say the town of Yacolt was built atop a Klickitat tribal burial ground. Is this the source of such eerie occurrences? The stolen children story is probably the most often told legend explaining the origin of the town's name, though other versions have been passed down through tribal lore. All involve spirits and disappearing souls.

In one story young Klickitat lovers are forbidden by the girl's father to be together. The beautiful maiden wanders off into the dense woods in great despair, and she is never again seen by her family or tribe. The Klickitats frequently told stories of disappearing lovers, such as the legend of the beautiful woman who hid herself away in a cave for many years in order to keep peace between lovers who fought over her affections.

Another account involving a battle between the Klickitats and a neighboring Willamette-area tribe was told by a settler, J. P. Banzer:

First I shall tell you how Yacolt was named. This is as it was told to me by an Indian and perhaps as told to him by his father or grandfather, for they had no written history and stories were handed down from father to son. This section where we are now sitting was, in the long ago and even in my time, a spot where wild strawberries and blueberries grew in abundance. The Klickitat Indians claimed the field and made their annual pilgrimage here to gather berries. On one occasion they found a number of Wilamie Indians, as they called them. A fight started and all the Wilamies were massacred, as they thought, but an Indian girl escaped. The next year, when the Klickitats returned, they heard someone singing the Wilamie death song and saw a maiden disappear in the distance. Several times they heard her sing. They said she was a spirit, the ghost of her people. The word "spirit" in Indian tongue is Yacolt and that is the Indian version of the naming of this territory.

In spite of its reputation, the valley was a gathering place for local Klickitat, Cowlitz, Chinook, and area tribes. Other tribes journeyed over the Cascade Mountains or came inland from the coast to trade salmon, game, roots, berries, and baskets. The tribes were flourishing when they encountered Lewis and Clark in 1806. With the explorers and trappers came disease, and the area tribes suffered great loss from ensuing epidemics. The Klickitats and Cowlitz were nearly wiped out by disease at the beginning of the nineteenth century.

Early settlers to the valley also tell of unusual or occult-type experiences. Edgar Rotchy, a farmer and musician who donated his papers to the University of Washington, wrote of fellow citizens of the town of Yacolt who claimed to be followed about or harassed by witches. Another said he heard the voices of spirits speaking to him. Rotchy's writings also describe his own frightening encounters with unknown beasts:

Once we were awakened in the middle of the night by the screams of a wild beast that sounded like the yells and laughter of a demented man. I took my rifle; it was moonlight; I went to the field, but could not make up [sic] the animal . . . [I have] never heard anything like it ever afterward.

Later, at another time, a large beast came to the edge of the cleared land, and would utter a scream that sounded like a frightened colt. I took my rifle, and a lantern, but the beast had disappeared.

By far the most devastating event to happen in this haunted valley was the epic Yacolt Burn of 1902. Until the 2014 Carleton Fire, the Yacolt Burn stood alone as the largest forest fire in state history. Fires were commonly caused by loggers slashing and burning or farmers clearing fields. These fires were often fueled by winds that settlers called "devil winds." Devil winds blew up the Columbia River Gorge, drying out timber and fanning flames. No one ever knew the exact cause of the Yacolt Burn, though logging was suspected. The fire ravaged over 370 square miles, killed 38 people, and burned nearly 150 homes from September 11–13, 1902.

Survivors told of the skies turning so dark that lights had to be used round-the-clock over one hundred miles away. Ash fell from the skies over Portland, depositing a gray layer half an inch deep on the ground. A darkness engulfed cities as far away as Seattle. University of Washington president, Henry Schmitz, described: "One of the most vivid memories of my childhood is the utter darkness that fell on Seattle one late summer day in 1902

Aftermath of Yacolt Burn, 1902   US Forest Service, Clark County Historical
Museum

caused by the smoke of the Yacolt Burn. There was darkness so
complete that it necessitated lighting the city's gas street lights by
early afternoon."

Pioneer Sophus Jacobson told of fighting the blaze: "We
fought day and night, and during the day the smoke was so heavy
that we had to use lanterns to light our way. There was really no
difference in lighting between the day and the night, and it became
confusing as to which was which."

Klickitat legends give vivid descriptions of the devastation of
fires in the region, which could have predicted the carnage to come
in later years: "All the forests were burned away, leaving only black
snags and smoldering logs: the berries, fruits, and camas, as well as
the maize patches, were destroyed. All the game had been killed or

driven out to a far country; most of the villages had been burned. The people had fled, been destroyed or were hiding in caves."

Witnesses to the Yacolt Burn told tales of death and survival. Livestock were cooked where they stood. A logger returning to camp after the fire found a group of pigs intact, standing upright on their feet, having been baked alive. People and animals ran for their lives; some made it, others did not. A mother attempted to shield her four children from the flames by sheltering the family in an underground cellar on their property. The family was smothered to death in the intense heat, but only fifty feet from them a grove of green alder trees was left untouched by the fire and would have offered them safe haven.

Farmers and settlers hitched up their wagons and rode from the flames as fast as they could while live embers fell all around them. A family of eleven on a picnic outing were all killed when their wagons were engulfed by the firestorm. People thought the end of the world had come. An early area settler reported:

In 1902, we had a terrible forest fire along here. Many people were burned to death. Many trees fell across the road and blocked the way out. We were hemmed in here and couldn't get out. We sat in our yard with our grips packed from Monday night until Saturday morning expecting every day to be burned to death. We laid on the ground most of the time and we kept the babies there all the time, because the only air one could breathe was next to the ground.

Men who had been prospecting, hunting, or fishing near a lake hastily built rafts upon which they floated for two straight days and nights. They had to continuously paddle to the center of the lake to avoid the flames raging on shore.

Small groups of the fifty or so citizens of Yacolt survived by sheltering in a nearby creek overnight. When they saw the burn coming at them from over the hill, they jumped into wagons and headed for the nearest water, where they survived by covering themselves with wet blankets while surrounded by fire and choking on the thick smoke. The blaze came within a half mile of the town, which was spared when the wind suddenly shifted. The heat was great enough to melt paint from the sides of buildings, but miraculously, most stood unharmed in the aftermath of the burn.

The fire that had burned thirty-six miles in thirty-six hours was finally halted by rain. The devastating aftermath was described in the local newspaper, *The Columbian*, on September 17, 1902: "What a week ago was the beautiful valley of the Lewis River is now a hot and silent valley of death, spotted with the blackened bodies of both man and beast."

Yacolt recovered, partly due to the burn, when a man named Frederick Weyerhaeuser started logging companies in the area to profit from salvaging the acres of fallen timber. These endeavors led to a Northwest timber dynasty and employed loggers for years to come. The town and valley experienced a relative population boom that ebbed and flowed until Yacolt became what it is now: a quiet, rural community where the residents sometimes see spirits, hear the ghosts of children laughing and footsteps on back stairways, or experience otherworldly sensations.

BIBLIOGRAPHY

D. B. COOPER, WHERE ARE YOU?

Boulé, Margie. "Other Theories on Cooper Parachute In." *The Oregonian*, 5 August 2004.

———. "Who Was D. B. Cooper? FBI Theories, New Evidence Revealed in Documentary." *The Oregonian*, 27 July 2004.

Carter, Mike and Steve Miletich. "Woman Is Sure Uncle was Fabled D. B. Cooper." *The Seattle Times*, 4 August 2011.

"Chute, It Wasn't D. B.'s." *Seattle Post-Intelligencer*, 26 November 1988.

"Cooper Is No 'Robin Hood.'" *ALPA Pilot Bulletin*. Vol. 31, No. 1, January 1972.

Cooper, Matt. "D. B. Cooper Legend Back in the Money with Movie's Release." *The Register-Guard*, 14 August 2004.

"Cooper Money." AP, 28 February 1980.

"D. B. Cooper." AP, 14 February 1980.

"D. B. Cooper." AP, 15 February 1980.

"D. B. Cooper." *The Columbian*, 1989.

"A D. B. Cooper Theory." *Seattle Post-Intelligencer*, 18 December 1989.

"Eight Years Then Irony." *Washington Star-News*, 22 February 1980.

Finegold, Larry. Interview, 15 February 2015.

Himmelsbach, Ralph. Interview, 18 February 2005.

Himmelsbach, Ralph P. and Thomas K. Worcester. *NORJAK: The Investigation of D. B. Cooper.* West Linn, Oregon: Norjak Project, 1986.

Jabin, Clyde. "D. B. Cooper." UPI, 12 February 1980.

Jewett, Dave. "The Search Goes On for D. B. Cooper." *The Columbian*, 2 October 1995.

Lyke, M. L. "Agents Tie Skyjacker D. B. Cooper to Green Beret." *Seattle Post-Intelligencer*, 15 October 1991.

McNerthney, Casey. "FBI Says No DNA Match in D. B. Cooper Case." SeattlePI.com, 9 August 2011.

Miletich, Steve. "Did D. B. Cooper Survive Jump?" *The Seattle Times*, 2 August 2011.

———. "FBI Probes New Lead in D. B. Cooper Skyjacking." *The Seattle Times*, 1 August 2011.

Oppegaard, Brett. "D. B. Cooper—A Crime Immortalized by Time." *The Columbian*, 22 November 1996.

———. "Legendary Lore or, Did Prunes Kill the President." *The Columbian*, 18 January 1995.

Seven, Richard. "D. B. Cooper—Perfect Crime or Perfect Folly?" *The Seattle Times*, 17 November 1996.

United States v. Fonseca-Machado, 53 F.3d 1242 (11th Cir. 1995).

"Why N.J. Murder Suspect Might Be D. B. Cooper." *Seattle Post-Intelligencer*, 30 June 1989.

DEMONS OF THE DEEP

Bille, Matthew A. *Rumors of Existence*. Surrey, British Columbia: Hancock House Publishers Ltd., 1995.

"An Electric Monster." *Tacoma Daily Ledger*, 2 July 1893.

Heuvelmans, Bernard, D.Sc., F.Z.S. *In the Wake of Sea-Serpents*. New York: Hill and Wang, 1968.

Johnson, Pauline E. *Legends of Vancouver*. Toronto: McClelland & Stewart, 1922.

LeBlond, Paul H. "Sea-Serpents of the Pacific Northwest." *Great Mysteries of the West*. Golden, Colorado: Fulcrum Publishing, 1993.

LeBlond, Paul H. and John Sibert. "Observations of Large Unidentified Marine Animals in British Columbia and Adjacent Waters," University of British Columbia, Institute of Oceanography, Vancouver, British Columbia, MS Rep. No. 28, 1973.

"Yachtsmen Tell of Huge Sea Serpent Seen off Victoria." *Victoria Daily Times*, 5 October 1933.

LEGEND OF THE TWO SADDLES TREASURE

Brown, Joseph C. *The Night the Mountain Fell*. Wenatchee, Washington: A KPQ Publication, 1973.

Dow, Edson. *Passes to the North, History of Wenatchee Mountains*. Wenatchee, Washington: Edson Dow, 1963.

Hackenmiller, Tom. *Wapato Heritage*. Manson, Washington: Point Publishing, 1995.

"Lost Treasure of the Trinidad—the Cached Gold." *Tri-City Herald*, 26 September 1968.

"Lost Welch Treasure." *Seattle Post-Intelligencer*, 1971.

Wenatchee Daily World, 30 September 1921.

THE GEORGETOWN CASTLE

Anderson, Rick. "Ghost Stories, Early Enough to Get Really Scared." *The Seattle Times*, 26 October 1987.

Anderson, Rick. "It's Time to Conjure Up Tales of Ghosts and Goblins." *The Seattle Times*, 29 October 1990.

Arnold, William. "Horrors That Haunt the Northwest." *Seattle Post-Intelligencer*, 31 October 1976.

Conklin, Ellis E. "Ghostly Encounters." *Seattle Post-Intelligencer*, 28 October 1997.

Easton, Valerie. "Haunted Now Back To Life." *The Seattle Times*, 28 October 2012.

"Georgetown, Public Art & Culture Walking Tour Map." Seattle Arts Commission, City of Seattle, 2004.

Lind, Carol. *Western Gothic*. Tumwater, Washington: Carol Lind, 1983.

McWade, Ray. Letter, 17 June 2004.

Pettersen, Petter. Interview, 23 May 2004.

MOUNTAIN DEVILS ON MOUNT ST. HELENS

Barham, Melvin, "Isabel Arcasa Keeps Indian Heritage Alive." *Wenatchee World*, 23 November 1980.

Beck, R. A. *I Fought the Apemen of Mt. St. Helens*. Kelso, Washington: 1967.

Byrne, Peter. *The Search for BIG FOOT Monster, Myth or Man?* Washington, D.C.: Acropolis Books Ltd., 1975.

Green, John. *On the Track of the Sasquatch*. Agassiz, British Columbia: Cheam Publishing Ltd., 1968.

———. *Sasquatch the Apes among Us*. British Columbia: Cheam Publishing Ltd./Hancock House Publishers, 1978.

Jacobs, Melville. "Northwest Sahaptin Texts." Columbia University Contributions to Anthropology, (1934) 29:1.

LADY OF THE LAKE

Conklin, Ellis E. "The Lady of the Lake, Tale of the Corpse Turned to Soap Keeps Lake Crescent Bubbling with Intrigue." *Seattle Post-Intelligencer*, 30 October 1990.

"Extradition of Bus Driver Sought." *Long Beach Independent*, 2 November 1941.

Fish, Harriet U. *Fish Tales of Lake Crescent*. Port Angeles, Washington: Fish Publication, 1985.

Fultz, Hollis B. "The Corpse That Came Back." *True Detective*, 1942.

"Illingworth in Washington to Face Charge of Strangling Wife to Death." *Long Beach Independent*, 7 November 1941.

McCallum, John D. *Crime Doctor*. Mercer Island, WA: The Writing Works, Inc., 1978.

Miller, Ray. "Monty Illingworth Faces Chain of Events Unearthed by Criminologist." *Long Beach Independent*, 31 October 1941.

Valadez, Jamie. "Native American Legends from the Olympic Peninsula." Port Angeles, Washington: Lower Elwha S'Kallam Tribe, Manuscript, 1988.

A WORLD-FAMOUS LOBOTOMY

Adcock, Joe. "'Frances' The Beautiful Movie Star from West Seattle Is Dead." *Seattle Post-Intelligencer*, 28 June 1983.

Arnold, William. *Shadowland*. New York: McGraw-Hill Book Company, 1978.

Carter, Don. "As 'Frances' Plays across the Land, $20 Million Suit against Filmmakers Waits in Wings." *Seattle Post-Intelligencer*, 28 January 1983.

El-Hai, Jack. "The Lobotomist." *The Washington Post*, 4 February 2001.

Elliot, Edith Farmer. *Look Back in Love*. Portland, Oregon: Gemaia Press, 1978.

"Ex-Seattle Girl Cries She 'Drank Everything.'" *The Seattle Times*, 14 January 1943.

Farmer, Frances. *Will There Really Be A Morning?* New York: Dell Publishing Co., 1972.

"Frances Farmer, 56, Former Actress, Dies." *The Seattle Times*, 3 August 1970.

"'Frances' Inaccurate, Say Former Nurses." *The Seattle Times*, 26 January 1983.

"Frances Farmer Put in Asylum." *The Seattle Times*, 24 March 1944.

"Frances Farmer Will Leave Hospital; May Do War Work." *The Seattle Times*, 2 July 1944.

Huston, Barbara. "'Frances' Opening Draws Crowds, Old Autos and a Star." *Seattle Post-Intelligencer*, 27 January 1983.

Tate, Cassandra. "Frances Farmer." HistoryLink.org, 17 January 2003.

Captain Ingalls's Gold

Brown, Joseph C. *The Night the Mountain Fell.* Wenatchee, Washington: A KPQ Publication, 1973.

Davenport, Marge. *Best of the Old Northwest.* Tigard, Oregon: Paddlewheel Press, 1980.

Dow, Edson. *Passes to the North, History of Wenatchee Mountains.* Wenatchee, Washington: Edson Dow, 1963.

Hackenmiller, Tom. *Wapato Heritage.* Manson, Washington: Point Publishing, 1995.

Palmer, Lucille. "Washington's Broken Mountain." Interview, November 1974.

Peterson, Susan. "A Beach of Gold Nuggets—A Mysterious Story." *Cascade Lookout.* Okanogan and Wenatchee National Forests: U.S. Forest Service (2003): 20.

Woods, Rufus. "The Story by Moses Splawn." *Wenatchee Daily World*, 7 June 1932 and 16 August 1932.

———. "Three Glamorous Decades in the Great Northwest." *Wenatchee Daily World*, 7 June 1932.

SHANGHAIED!

"Boy Disappears from Home." *Seattle Post-Intelligencer*, 4 January 1901.

"Boys Escape Clutches of Crimps—Lads Who Swam Ashore to Avoid Being Carried to Sea." *The Seattle Times*, 27 November 1905.

"Brothers, Fathers, Husbands." *The Seattle Star*, 4 January 1901.

"Jump Overboard to Escape From Ship." *Seattle Post-Intelligencer*, 27 November 1905.

McDonald, Lucile. "A Captain Usually Got His Crew in Port Townsend's Uninhibited Past." *The Seattle Times*, 9 September 1962.

Newell, Gordon. *Sea Rogues' Gallery*. Seattle: Superior Publishing Company, 1971.

The Seattle Star, 3 January 1901.

"Shanghaied Sailor Comes Back." *The Seattle Times*, 13 July 1908.

Simpson, Peter. *City of Dreams, a Guide to Port Townsend*. Port Townsend: The Bay Press, 1986.

FLYING SAUCERS OVER MOUNT RAINIER

Arnold, Kenneth. *The Coming of the Saucers*. Boise, ID: self-published, 1953.

Bequette, Bill. AP, 25 June 1947.

"Flying Disc Mystery Grows; Many See 'em." *The Tacoma News Tribune*, 28 June 1947.

Gibbs, William E. "The Roswell Incident, an 'Unsolved' or 'Unsolvable' Mystery?" *Great Mysteries of the West*. Golden, Colorado: Fulcrum Publishing, 1993.

Jacobs, David M. *The UFO Controversy*. Bloomington: Indiana University Press, 1975.

Maccabee, Bruce. *The FBI-UFO Connection*. Minneapolis, Minnesota: Llewellyn Publishing, 2000.

———. *June 24, 1947: How It All Began*. Grand Rapids, Michigan: Manuscript of Presentation at Symposium of the Mutual UFO Network. 12 July 1997.

Michel, Aime. "The First Reports." *The Truth about Flying Saucers*. New York: Criterion Books, 1956.

Peebles, Curtis. "The Age of Confusion Begins." *Watch the Skies! A Chronicle of the Flying Saucer Myth*. Washington and London: The Smithsonian Institution Press, 1994.

"Seattle Lensman First to 'Catch' Disk by Camera," *Seattle Post-Intelligencer*, 5 July 1947.

Skiff, Nolan. *East Oregonian*, 25 June 1947.

"What Was It? Wonderful Apparition Seen over Tacoma." *The Tacoma Daily Ledger*, 27 November 1896.

The Mad Doctor's South Hill Mansion

Clark, Doug. "For Sale: Spooky South Hill Mansion with a Wild, Bloody Past." *The Spokesman-Review*, 3 March 1991.

———. "UI Student Scares Up Thesis Data." *The Spokesman-Review*, 13 August 1991.

Ditto, Frank and Stephanie. Wilbur-Hahn House—Nomination Form, Spokane Register of Historic Places. Spokane City-County Historic Preservation Department, 4 January 1993.

"Dr. Hahn Former Barber." *The Spokesman-Review*, 5 December 1929.

"Dr. Hahn Freed of Prison Term." *The Spokesman-Review*, 23 June 1945.

"Dr. Hahn's Wife Is Found Slain." *The Spokesman-Review*, 3 May 1940.

"French Bayonet in Heart." *The Spokesman-Review*, 7 August 1946.

Guilfoil, Michael. "Restoring 'Ghostly' House Requires Lots of TLC." *The Spokesman-Review*, 30 October 1992.

"Historic Mansion Bought for Aged." *The Spokesman-Review*, 25 May 1945.

Holbrook, Stewart H. *The Golden Age of Quackery*. New York: The MacMillan Company, 1959.

"Home May Drop Saga of Sorrow." *The Spokesman-Review*, 29 May 1945.

STRANGE STEILACOOM

Clements, Barbara and Gestin Suttle. "They Lurk, They Stomp, They Haunt Many Ghosts Apparently Call Tacoma Area Home." *The News Tribune*, 31 October 1996.

Meeker, Ezra. *Pioneer Reminiscences of Puget Sound*. Seattle: Ezra Meeker, 1905.

Merryman, Kathleen. "Historic Haunts: Along the Streets of Steilacoom Linger Memories—and Maybe More Than That—of Dead Residents." *The News Tribune*, 31 October 1992.

———. "The Spirit of Steilacoom." *The News Tribune*, 31 October 1991.

———. "With a Gentle Nudge, History Topples Over into Mystery." *The News Tribune*, 30 October 2000.

"The Murder." *Puget Sound Herald*, 29 January 1863.

Prosch, Charles. "Death of Albert G. Balch." *Puget Sound Herald*, 1 January 1863.

Robinson, Sean. "Psychics of Soul Searching." *The News Tribune*, 31 October 2002.

"The Strange Story of Albert Balch." *Steilacoom Historical Museum Quarterly*, XI (Spring 1982): p. 9.

Vaughn, William D. "The Byrd Murder." *Tacoma Weekly Ledger*, 17 February 1893.

Voelpel, Dan. "Frighteningly Good Pasta? There's a Reason." *The News Tribune*, 1 November 2004.

THE EARL OF BLEWETT PASS

Bailey, Kate. "Hoard of Gold Coins Hid in Blewett Pass Region?" *Wenatchee World*, 28 June 1956.

Brown, Joseph C. *The Night the Mountain Fell*. Wenatchee, Washington: A KPQ Publication, 1973.

Dow, Edson. *Passes to the North, History of the Wenatchee Mountains*. Wenatchee, Washington: Edson Dow, 1963.

The Imperial Gazetteer of Scotland. Edinburgh, Scotland: 1859.

In the Matter of the Estate of Thomas Douglas, Deceased, Cause Number 108. The Superior Court of the State of Washington, in and for the County of Chelan, 18 March 1905.

Jameson, W.C. *Buried Treasures of the Pacific Northwest*. Little Rock, Arkansas: August House Publishers, Inc., 1995.

MADCAP MAY'S CURSE

"Former Lady Hope, Actress, Who Once Had World at Her Feet, Works As Janitress in a Seattle Shipyard." *Seattle Post-Intelligencer*, 24 November 1918.

Fowler, Marian. *Adventures of a Diamond*. New York: Ballantine, 2002.

Gates, H. L. and May Yohe. *The Mystery of the Hope Diamond*. New York: International Copyright Bureau, 1921.

"May Yohe Asks for a Divorce—Bane of Great Hope Diamond Seems to Fall on All Its Possessors." *Seattle Post-Intelligencer*, 10 March 1910.

McLean, Evalyn Walsh. *Father Struck It Rich*. Boston: Little, Brown and Company, 1936.

Newell, Gordon and Don Sherwood. *Totem Tales of Old Seattle*. New York: Ballantine Books, 1974.

Patch, Susan. *Blue Mystery, the Story of the Hope Diamond*. Washington, D.C.: Smithsonian Institution Press, 1976.

"The Strange Case of May Yohe." *LIFE* magazine, 23 May 1938. Vol. 4, No. 21, p. 39.

KENNEWICK MAN

"Bones Are 9,000 Years Old." *The Seattle Times*, 28 August 1996.

Bonnichsen v. United States of America, 357 F.3d 962 (9th Cir. February 4, 2004).

Callaway, Ewen. "Ancient American Genome Rekindles Legal Row." *Nature*, 18 June 2015; vol. 522, issue 7557, 404–405.

Dietrich, Bill. "Ancient Bones, Ancient Disputes—Is Kennewick Skeleton 'Asian' or 'European'? *The Seattle Times*, 29 August 1996.

Dietrich, Bill. "Skeleton Might Be Reburied Before Scientists Can Study It." *The Seattle Times*, 22 September 1996.

Doughton, Sandi. "Kennewick Man's DNA Likely That of a Native." *The Seattle Times*, 18 January 2015.

———. "Tantalizing Find." *The Seattle Times*, 16 May 2014.

Frazier, Joseph B. "Scientists Can Study Kennewick Remains." AP, 5 February 2004.

Geranios, Nicholas K. "Kennewick Man: Figure of Dispute, Mystery—Scientists, Tribes at Odds over Prehistoric Remains." AP, 10 August 1997.

Gugliotta, Guy. "'Kennewick Man': No Ethnic Match— Scientists Say Skull Doesn't Fit in with Traits of Modern Populations." *The Washington Post*, 27 July 1999.

Henderson, Diedtra. "Kennewick Man: A Closer Look—a Window of Time—in Studying the Site Where Kennewick Man Was Found, Scientists Hope to Learn More About an Ancient Skeleton and about a People 'Essentially Forgotten to History.'" *The Seattle Times*, 16 December 1997.

———. "Kennewick Man Study Begins Today." *The Seattle Times*, 25 February 1999.

"Judge's Ruling Limits Kennewick Man Suit." *The Seattle Times*, 19 August 2004.

Mapes, Lynda V. "Treasured Skeleton Not Local, Scientist Tells Tribes." *The Seattle Times*, 10 October 2012.

McManamon, Francis P. "K-Man Undergoes Complete Physical." *Anthropology Newsletter*, American Anthropological Association. Arlington, Virginia: May 1999.

Sorensen, Eric. "Kennewick Man's Age Confirmed: 9,300 and Counting." *The Seattle Times*, 13 January 2000.

Stang, John. "Skull Found on Shore of Columbia." *Tri-City Herald*, 29 July 1996.

"Tribes Ask U.S. Court to Halt Skeleton Study." *The Seattle Times*, 11 September 2004.

HEXED

Dunkelberger, Steve. "Terrified in Tacoma." *Tacoma Weekly*. 23 July 2013.

Harper, Larry. "Bird Guilty, Will Hang." *Tacoma News Tribune*. 27 November 1947.

"Fifth Man in Bird's 'Hex' Dies." *Tacoma News Tribune*. 29 November 1948.

"Jake Bird Hangs for Ax Murders." *Tacoma News Tribune*. 15 July 1949.

"Widow and Daughter Slain with Ax." *Tacoma News Tribune*. 30 October 1947.

McCallum, John D. *Crime Doctor*. Mercer Island, WA: The Writing Works, Inc., 1978.

McClary, Daryl C. "Police Capture Serial Killer Jake Bird after He Murders Two Tacoma Women on October 30, 1947." (historylink.org) 5 October 2006. Accessed 16 March 2015.

YACOLT—VALLEY OF EVIL SPIRITS

"The Big Fire of 1902." *Washington Pioneer Project*. Told by the Pioneers. Olympia, Washington: Office of the Secretary of State, 1938.

Bunnell, Clarence Orvel. *Legends of the Klickitats*. Portland, Oregon: Metropolitan Press, 1935.

Caldbick, John. "Yacolt—Thumbnail History." (historylink.org) 14 March 2010.

"Clark Brown Visits." *Trail Breakers*. Clark County Historical Society. Vol. 34, July 2007 to June 2008: 60–61.

Daugherty, Cheryl. "The Yacolt Burn of 1903." *Clark County History*. Vancouver, Washington: Vancouver Historical Society, 1991.

Holbrook, Stewart. "The Yacolt Burn." *The Columbia*. New York, New York: Rinehart & Co., 1956.

Olson, Joan and Gene. "The Day of the Dragon." *Washington Times and Trails*. Grants Pass, Oregon: Windyridge Press, 1970.

Oppegaard, Brett. "Simply Supernatural or, Getting in the Spirit of Things." *The Columbian*, 15 January 1995.

Rotschy, Edgar. "Early Days in Yacolt." Unpublished
  Autobiography, Edgar Rotschy Papers, 1892–1933. University
  of Washington Special Collections.

Vorenberg, Sue. "Small Town Big on Spirits: A Haunting in
  Yacolt?" *The Columbian*, 29 October 2011.

Wilma, David. "Yacolt Burn, Largest Forest Fire in Recorded
  Washington History to that Point, Rages from September 11
  to September 13, 1902." (historylink.org) 14 February 2003.

———. "Yacolt to Hear from J. P. Banzer the Legend of How
  Yacolt Got Its Name." *The Columbian*, 18 April 1938.

"Yacolt Washington—History." Town of Yacolt, Washington.
  (townofyacolt.com). Accessed 5 November 2014.

INDEX

ABOUT THE AUTHOR

L. E. Bragg is a Washington State native whose books about the Pacific Northwest include: *More than Petticoats: Remarkable Washington Women* and *More than Petticoats: Remarkable Idaho Women,* and the picture books *A River Lost, Heart of the Palús,* and *Seattle, City by the Sound.* She lives near Seattle.